FALLACIES OF WOMEN'S LIBERATION

Robert D. McCracken

Dedication

I dedicate this book to the Women's Liberationists; their plethora of nonsense and misinformation has provided me with the motivation to write it.

FALLACIES
OF
WOMEN'S
LIBERATION

Robert D. McCracken

Shields Publishing, Inc.
855 Broadway ● P.O. Box 1917
Boulder, Colorado 80302

44473

Fallacies of Women's Liberation

Library of Congress Catalog Card Number: 72-89863
International Standard Book Number; 0-88310-000-2

Acknowledgements

Grateful acknowledgement is made to the publishers and authors who granted permission to use the following selections and illustrations

From "Interview with Germaine Greer," *Penthouse Magazine,* September, 1971. Copyright 1971 by Penthouse—©Penthouse International Ltd. Reprinted by permission of the publisher.

From *"Playboy* Interview: Germaine Greer" (January, 1972); copyright © 1971 by *Playboy,* Used with permission.

Excerpts from "Sisterhood Is Beautiful, A Conversation with Alice S. Rossi" by Gordon Bermant, *Psychology Today* Magazine, August, 1972. Copyright © Communications/Research/Machines, Inc.

From the Introduction to *Sisterhood Is Powerful: An Anthology of Writings from the Women's Liberation Movement,* Robin Morgan, ed. Copyright © 1970 by Random House, Inc. Reprinted by permission of the publisher.

From *Sexual Politics* by Kate Millett. Copyright © 1971 by Doubleday and Co. Reprinted by permission of the publisher.

From "The Nature and Evolution of Female Sexuality" by Mary Jane Sherfey in *Sisterhood Is Powerful: An Anthology of Writings from the Women's Liberation Movement,* Robin Morgan, ed. Copyright © 1970 by Random House, Inc. Reprinted by permission of the publisher.

Preface

My thanks to the many scholars and research scientists whose work I have cited in this volume. My brother, Michael McCracken, played a significant role in the development of many of the theories and ideas presented here. I gratefully acknowledge his assistance. Alice Levine deserves a special word of thanks for her help in the preparation of this manuscript. The assistance and patience of my wife, Susan, has proved to be invaluable. Ester McDowell and Meredith Shields typed drafts of this manuscript.

My thanks to John Jellico and his students at the Colorado Institute of Art for all of the art work contained in this volume. Richard R. Murray designed the cover. Others in order of appearance: Ed Isakson, Rick Gentry, Jerry Fogg, Dean Doss, Jim Oblander, Barry Spoon, Daune Britton, and Joyce Leadbetter.

Robert D. McCracken

Contents

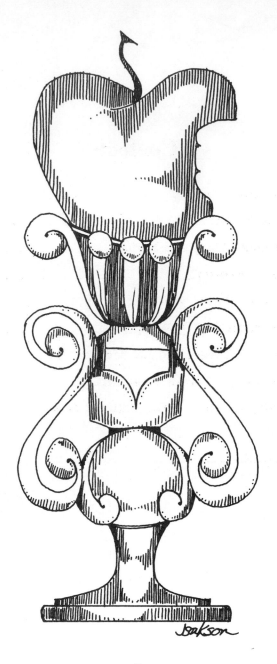

Introduction

Women burn their bras in the streets. Gloria Steinem searches Manhattan for a "hotel owned by women" and complains that she cannot find one. The first regular issue of *Ms.* magazine, unofficial house organ of the Women's Liberation movement, features a cartoon of Wonder Woman on the cover. In that issue a woman states that she did not choose "man hating," but that "man hating" chose her. Two lesbians portray homosexual love in sympathetic terms. Germaine Greer announces that she does not own a bra or girdle and that she has stopped wearing panties. An unemployed, childless graduate student demands that her husband, who is a college professor, do half the housework, cooking, and shopping and that he get out of the house one night each week in order that she may hold consciousness-raising meetings with her Liberationist friends. Housewives contend that they work over 90 hours a week and are entitled to at least $10,000 a year in payment for that work. A large protest is directed against a major airline that features a pretty stewardess and a suggestive slogan in company advertising. Linguists propose banishing all pronouns that designate gender from the English language.

I sometimes find it difficult to take Women's Liberationists seriously. Their capacity for clowning, the poor quality of their social theory and philosophy, the nonrepresentativeness of its members and their supporters, the strutting and flamboyance of its leaders, the slovenliness and negativism of many of its members make it highly uncharacteristic of most of the great or even modest social movements of the past.

While many aspects of Women's Liberation are laughable and undoubtedly transitory, the movement should be examined. From an anthropological perspective, deep social forces power the Women's Liberationist movement. (The origin of these forces is discussed in detail in Chapter 1.) Socio-historical forces create social movements, such as Women's Liberation. But the specific form that a movement takes and many of its features are shaped and controlled by individuals. Two groups of individuals have had an especially pronounced effect on the Women's Liberation movement. One is the media; the other is made up of those individuals who have emerged as leaders.

The role that the media has played in the shaping of the Women's Liberation movement is not the topic of this volume, and will be treated only in passing. The movement has been and will continue to be centered in two places: New York City and the liberal college campuses.

Nearly all of the big publishing houses in this country are headquartered in New York. The same city is the center of the national TV networks, the newspaper and wire services, and the film industry. While there is probably minimal interaction between the leaders of these specific industries, the personnel who make the decisions in each specific industry constitute little more than a fraternity headquartered and housed in New York City. As a consequence, a similarity of world view pervades the leadership, and probably the staff workers as well, of each of these industries. Their frame of reference for judging the world becomes New York and the New Yorkers they work and live with.

The new editors of *Saturday Review* were aware of this insulation when they decided to move their main office from New York to San Francisco. In an editorial explaining the move they described the media's concentration in New York.

> The headquarters of the three commercial television networks are within slingshot range of one another. The two leading American wire services are a dozen blocks

apart. Most of the nation's leading book publishers are
in New York, and all but a handful of America's major
magazines are put out in Manhattan. There is such an
incredible concentration of editors, writers, researchers,
publishers, literary agents, and advertising men around
midtown that one could transact all of his business
within a radius of one mile, or less. This can, and does,
lead to a good deal of fruitful cross-fertilization. But it
can, and does, also lead to a certain amount of
inbreeding — and parochialism. (*Saturday Review,* Sept.
2, 1972, p. 24)

As a result of this geographic concentration, the media
(perhaps with no deliberate intent) portrays New York as the
Mecca of America and the center of civilization. New
Yorkers who control the media have assumed that all
Americans, from Duluth to Baton Rouge, from Montgomery
to Pocatello, believe what they believe, and want to hear what
they have to say. But this is not true. America listens because
there is no other slickly packaged voice. They do not believe;
they do not agree. The liberal dominated media centered in
New York City is seriously out of touch with many of things
that are now taking place in America.

New York City, the headquarters of the media, was one of
the centers of Women's Liberation, so it was natural for the
media to publicize and direct attention toward this movement. Since the members of the media came from the same
social class and were educated in the same elite liberal
colleges as the liberationists, they were probably also more
than sympathetic. A flood of stories sympathetic to the
movement began to pour out of New York City in magazines
and books, on TV, radio, and even film. There was never a
balanced point of view. The other side of the story of the
Women's Liberation movement has never been presented by
any of the media. My survey of the literature dealing with
Women's Liberation has revealed scarcely a single news story
or magazine article and only two books (Norman Mailer's
and Midge Decter's) out of the literally thousands of
references that try to deal with negative aspects of Women's

Liberation. The media's blitz of propaganda dealing with Women's Liberation is probably one of the most extensive and one-sided in this century. The only comparable one in the last twenty years would be the media's continued, but diminishing vilification of the Southern states on the civil rights issue.

One of the most significant, yet least realized results of the media's one-sided presentation of the Women's Liberation issue is the negative effect that it has had on the self-image of the average mother and housewife. Most people would probably agree that if a woman is not forced to work because of family economics, there is no more important task in society than homemaking and proper care of children. Because of the media's incessant publicizing of the Women's Liberationists' complaints the role of housewife and mother are constantly being degraded. The effect of the media's degradation of women's traditional way of life is that of a self-fullfilling prophesy: formerly motherhood and homemaking were not seen as degrading; but now that prestigious information sources have said so loudly that it is, it has become so. The irony is that the effect has been the opposite of that intended. A vocal dissatisfied minority of women with ample assistance from the media attempted to "liberate" their sisters; in their efforts to liberate the majority, they degraded their way of life and destroyed their self-image.

Another wellspring of the Women's Liberation movement is found in the large public supported state universities and the small elite private colleges and universities. Leftist-oriented liberal arts faculties continually present honest but frequently one-sided views of society and its problems. For reasons I do not completely understand, students are quite receptive to these views and are willing to act on them. Protests in general, but especially those involving students and ethnic minorities, represent prime news sources to the media. Thus coverage is assured. The wide media coverage of

4

the Women's Liberationists on campuses presents the illusion that the movement has more substance and is more widespread than it actually is.
I would now like to turn to the purpose of this volume, namely an analysis of some of the more substantive issues that the Women's Liberationists have raised. However, it is necessary to define the term Women's Liberationist. As presently constituted in this country, the women's rights movement is extremely diverse; it is characterized by a great deal of heterogeneity among the individuals who in one way or another support it. For example, a Women's Liberationist might be seen as any woman, or perhaps man, who is dissatisfied with the current life style of women, and might range from the young housewife who dislikes washing dirty diapers but complains only to herself to the most hardened and bitter male-hating lesbian who flaunts her predicament to the world. While it is *possible* to include both these individuals under the general heading of "Women's Liberationist," we would have far too broad a concept to be of much use in discussing the major theoretical points that the liberationists have been raising. Something a good deal more specific is needed.
A second way to arrive at a definition of a Women's Liberationist would be to survey all women who consider themselves in sympathy with the movement, and analyze the data. While such a project would tell us a good deal about the composition of the movement in this country, it would be of little aid in an analysis of the issues raised by the movement.
In view of the shortcomings of the above methods, I believe the best way to proceed with an analysis of the thoughts and programs of the Women's Liberation movement is to examine what the leaders of the movement have said and written. Their works and statements are a matter of public record. If the Women's Liberationists cannot be judged in terms of what its leaders say and do, then there is, in effect, no public accountability of the movement itself, and the

movement loses the very element that all members would agree is the basis of their actions in the first place, namely justice.

An examination of the written and spoken statements emanating from the Women's Liberation movement shows that several serious problems and fallacies plague their thoughts and deeds. In Chapter 1 I have attempted to show that the very act of becoming a member of any social movement, including Women's Liberation, involves an intellectual compromise. Strong commitment to any ideology necessarily involves intellectual rigidity and a loss of sense of humor, increased irrationality and emotionalism, and a division of the world into friend and foe. In this chapter I have also attempted to sketch the socio-historical origins of the Women's Liberation movement (the leaders appear to be completely ignorant of this subject). I also attempt to demonstrate that Women's Liberation is a middle-class phenomena and its leaders tend to view the world in terms of that class. In Chapter 2, some of the complaints and proposals of Women's Liberation are examined. A theory for the interaction between behavior and human evolution is formulated and the origin of the human family, the value of male dominance and the traditional pattern of the division of labor are viewed in this light. In Chapter 3 the assertion that there are few innate behavioral differences between men and women is examined in the light of a large body of literature from the medical, biological, anthropological, and psychological sciences. The development of adult femininity and masculinity is also reviewed and it is suggested that it is biologically and psychologically much more difficult to become a normally functioning male. In Chapter 4 it is suggested that the Women's Liberationists have misanalyzed the role of the adult female in American society. Far from being exploited, middle-class American females constitute a pampered privileged class the likes of which the world has seldom seen.

In Chapter 5 the contention that the Women's Liberationist movement is progressive is challenged. Close examination of the words and deeds of the liberationists reveals that far from being progressive, it is highly reactionary and constitutes in its present form a massive rip-off by middle-class women of professional jobs. In Chapter 6 some of the shenanigans that the Women's Liberationists are playing with the English language are examined. In Chapter 7 the implications and prospects for success of the so-called Equal Rights Amendment are examined. In Chapter 8 the author's belief in the value of American masculine culture is reaffirmed.

The intellectual validity and the social worth of the Women's Liberationist movement must stand or fall on its words and deeds. There is, however, no guarantee that social movements with sterling intellectual and moral credentials will succeed and those based on foolishness and ignorance will fail; in fact often the reverse seems to be true. The world of the intellect, the world of truth, is a thing apart from success, however, and no amount of social success, no amount of manipulation can turn a fallacy into a truth and no cosmetic can transform a fool into a wiseman. I cannot predict what success the Women's Liberationist movement will ultimately have. I suspect that, like the ripples from a stone thrown in a still pond, the effect will be noticeable at first; but as the turbulence moves across the surface, the energy will be absorbed and in a few years the effect will be scarcely discernible. In another generation, even a hundred years from now, the nuclear family will be intact; women will still have babies; the mothers of the babies will still be primarily responsible for their care; women will still do most of the housework; and most women will still submit to the primeval moral authority of the male. More women will be working and more will regret it, looking back at the good deal they once had. Men will still make most of the important decisions in society; men will still be the inventors; men will still go to war; men will still be doing the dirty, back-breaking jobs that need to get done in a society; men will still have a shorter life expectancy than women; men will still run the 100-yard dash and the mile faster than women; and a male will still quarterback the Dallas Cowboys.

1

Is It A Revolt?

—Louis XVI

Characteristics

While driving to the West Coast, three coeds from prestigious Eastern colleges generously gave a lift to a male hitchhiker who was also returning home from school. The coeds found their new traveling companion to be an asset to the journey. When the group stopped for gasoline, the hitchhiker purchased a copy of *Playboy Magazine* and began reading it as they drove away. The girls said nothing and exhibited no overt signs of disapproval. At last, however, he chuckled aloud at a joke. The driver of the automobile immediately pulled the car off the road and stopped. "I will not ride in the same car with a male chauvinist pig," she announced. In an effort to apologize, save his ride, and lighten the tension, the hitchhiker responded, "It was a political joke." No one laughed and the young man was without a lift.

The story illustrates several characteristics of the Women's Liberation movement: the loss of a sense of humor, irrationality and emotionalism, and divisiveness.

The loss of a sense of humor is apparently an essential trait of all social movements. It is characteristic of both the far Right and Left, of religious movements, of the environmentalists, and of the food fadists; in the past it was seen in both the abolitionists and slaveholders. Loss of the ability to see oneself or one's situation in a humorous manner probably indicates a high degree of ego involvement. When self-identity becomes so enwrapped in a concept or a set of propositions that one cannot temporarily divorce oneself from their import and meaning, then one loses the ability to view the absurdity and the folly that is inherent in all human situations. As one becomes deeply committed to a social movement or a cause, a general rigidity seems to set in, and ultimately one loses one's sense of humor. At such times the individual finds it more and more difficult to laugh at any kind of humorous situation with the possible exception of a few esoteric in-group jokes. The girls in the anecdote will not allow the humor of an off-color joke because they have wholeheartedly committed themselves to a new doctrine that does not accept the fact that the members of virtually every cultural group in the world find humor in male-female sexuality.

Second, the story illustrates the irrationality and emotionalism that characterizes all social movements including Women's Liberation. The young man had not deliberately offended the girls; offense was probably the farthest thing from his mind. But the girls were so imbued with their self-righteous beliefs they could not see the situation as humorous. Instead of laughing with the young man, or at least ignoring him, the girls responded with the same sort of intolerance and rigidity that Women's Liberationists contend they are protesting. The girls were behaving in the same heavy-handed manner that they attribute to their "male oppressors." They could see and respond to only one aspect of the entire situation. Their repertoire of responses had become restricted. Reformers inevitably profess commitment to higher principles of justice, but when they become the administrators of justice, it is a matter of administering it in terms of power and not the high ideals they originally professed.

Third, the story illustrates how social movements frequently create division between groups. Rather than providing a basis of unity, as their rhetoric so often professes, Women's Liberationists are splitting asunder and destroying an already narrow avenue of communication between the sexes. Instead of encouraging a physical and psychological liaison of the sexes, their rhetoric and actions are dividing society into two more polarized camps. Men and women have been programmed by hundreds of millions of years of biological evolution to enjoy one another's company. The program tape however is fragile and can be twisted easily. Hostility generated by the commitment of these new Puritans to unthinking dogma can do little to facilitate the union of men and women. It can only lead to more suspicion and isolation.

Causes

What are the causes of the Women's Liberation movement? What are the social and historical forces behind it? Why have so many women suddenly become so dissatisfied? Why are women suddenly demanding freedom and liberation when for hundreds of generations there has been scarcely a whimper? Why do so many women now lament their lives, when in the past most of the women of most societies have been as content with their lives as most of the men of those societies.

The rhetoric of the movement does not necessarily provide the answer. If there is one thing that the behavioral sciences have established in the last fifty years, it is that the reasons individuals give for participating in social movements are not the same as the forces that actually cause the movement. Social movements originate from imperatives stemming from the society as a whole and not from private motives of individuals (White, 1949). This principle has been supported by studies of individuals who participate in wars and other forms of social upheavals. Examination of the individuals' motives for participating in social movements consistently reveals great variability; many of the motives do not have the remotest connection to the actual causes of the movement itself (Devereaux, 1961; Wallace, 1970). Individuals, including the leaders, who engage in such activities, while having their own private motives for participation, are from the view of the total society, pawns of vast socio-cultural imperatives, which they usually do not know exist and certainly do not comprehend. Men go to war to fight for freedom and honor, to win status among the folks at home—and because they are drafted; the wars themselves are caused by international competition for natural resources, trade routes and domination of foreign territories. Much the same kind of logic can be applied to the Women's Liberation movement. Women are motivated to participate because they feel "exploited" and because they want to be "liberated;" yet we must look elsewhere for the real causes. The real causes lie in the fact that technology and urbanization have forced us to alter the traditional division of work in our society.

Division of Labor in Society

In every society there is an absolute minimum of work that must be performed by the members of that society. In simple societies, failure to do such work, for example, making adequate provisions for food and shelter, can result in death to many if not all the members of the society. In more complex societies, a similar failure can result in serious social disruptions; if the failure is severe, death to members of the society can result. Recent strikes by garbage collectors and dock workers are illustrations of social disruptions; fatalities would result if hospitals and drug dispensaries were to completely shut down.

Throughout history all societies have recognized this essential feature of survival and have taken action to see that work gets done. In every society this has been accomplished through what has been called "division of labor." Certain members, and more importantly certain groups, within the society are assigned certain tasks. In all societies, especially the simpler ones such as hunters and gatherers, one of the most important features of the system of designation of work duty has been the division of labor according to sex. (Another is age.) That is to say, women as a group are assigned certain work tasks and men are assigned others. Often the work roles of the sexes overlap, but in no society are the roles assigned to the sexes interchangeable. In most societies female tasks are concerned with child care, collection and production of certain agricultural products, preparation of the food, and care of the family dwelling. Male tasks traditionally center about hunting, fishing, group defense, and religion. Regarding traditional societies, it is not possible to say that the duties of one sex are more important than the other, and conversely it is not possible to say that one set of duties is more trivial or demeaning than the other. All of the essential work must be performed or survival of the group will be threatened.

The manner in which traditional, slow changing societies divide up the labor is said to be "functional;" that is, it serves an important function in the smooth operation of the society. However, the division of labor that is functional in traditional societies (societies that are not undergoing rapid change), may not necessarily be functional in societies that are undergoing rapid change. This is especially true of complex, rapidly changing societies such as our own. When the traditionally assigned work role of a group ceases to be functional in a complex, rapidly changing society, a temporary social upheaval results. The group whose work role is becoming nonfunctional grows increasingly more dissatisfied with itself and the society; the society in turn becomes dissatisfied with the group. Social forces attempt to ameliorate the situation and bring the group back into social equilibrium through the evolution of new work roles. This situation has given rise to the movement called Women's

Liberation. (The division of labor will be discussed further in Chapter 2.)

Women in Early American Society

In frontier American society, women performed a vital role in household economy. Women's work was absolutely essential to the survival of the family. In a rural setting their economic duties centered about the production of life's necessities in the garden and home. In the garden and orchard they produced food. In the kitchen they canned fruit and vegetables. They made bread and pastries in ovens heated by wood they had gathered and chopped. They milked cows, tended chickens, and tanned hides from home-grown stock. The traditional American housewife produced a large percentage of the family's clothing and bedding, often from handmade fabrics. The chores of the frontier wife complemented the agricultural duties of the husband.

The construction of roads was one of the factors that began to undermine women's vital economic role. Adequate roads made possible the distribution of manufactured goods from central areas. Goods could be ordered through the catalog by the rural family and delivered over new roads. The ability to purchase clothes, bedding, utensils, and furniture soon relieved frontier women of the job of producing them. With this seemingly innocent beginning the burgeoning technology of American society rapidly destroyed the rural base of the American woman's economic productivity. The development of industry in urban centers encouraged migration of the more marginal farmers from rural to urban settings. Life in urban areas made the continuance of the American woman's productive role impossible. Lack of home-grown fruits and vegetables as well as the easy access to store-bought canned goods rendered impractical the former necessity of canning foods at home. Bread, or what came to pass for bread, and pastries became available at an economic price at the supermarket. Thus, a whole generation of women not only did not make bread; they did not even know how to. Gas and electric ovens, water heaters, washing machines, dryers, vacuum cleaners, and other electric appliances drastically cut into women's traditional work role. No longer did a woman make her children's clothing; no longer did she make quilts. These items could now be purchased for little more than the cost of the material. The eventual effect of the new technology was to make the American woman an economic fifth wheel.

There was one other important factor. While the husband had shifted relatively easily from his role as a rural agriculturist to an urban wage earner, his take-home wage did not provide enough cash for the family to buy all the products that the new technology offered and which advertising had convinced them they needed. Because of increased expenses it was necessary for the American housewife to supplement the family income through wage labor. She had to make up the economic loss suffered by the purchase of goods and services. The American woman was now forced to leave her home and sell her labor at least part-time on the job market.

Women in the Job Market

However, the job market had traditionally been an exclusive male domain — that is to say, employment in the job market had been the male's role in the division of labor. In the beginning most women did not like the idea of going to work on the job market; it was an insult to their female dignity. The men didn't like it either. It was also an insult to what had come to be known as their dignity. But unless men and women could somehow turn back the clock, terminate their affair with the new technology, and return to a rural way of life, there was nothing either could do about it. Both were controlled by economic and cultural forces.

Like any social group attempting to move into an area that is considered the exclusive domain of another group, the women attempting to define new roles on the job market met a good deal of resistance from men and women. They were forced to take the most menial jobs; they were rarely promoted to positions of decision-making and power; in short they were forced to compete with men when their whole tradition and historical experience had not equipped them for such competition. The men rationalized, with some validity, that the most important jobs required an employee's complete devotion, and women with children would always suffer from a division of loyalties; in the end, the children would come first. After all, had not seventy million years of mammalian evolution instilled in the human female some proclivity to love and nurture her children, if need be, at the expense of all other interests, even her own life?

The Birth of the Movement

As technology replaced the American female in the home and as women met resistance in their attempts to delineate new roles on the job market, some grumbling from both men and women could be heard. But in terms of any real social protest it was not significant. The blacks and the civil rights movement of the 1950s forged an effective and socially acceptable mode of protest. The blacks were followed by the Chicanos, the Indians, and other minorities. Dissatisfied women, seeing that white male culture had become vulnerable to protest and change adopted the methods of the minority groups and went on the attack.

Assisted by the media, the Women's Liberationist movement became very vocal and gained national prominence. Several books by Women's Liberationists reached the best seller list; the magazines, particularly those catering to women, were filled with talk of "sexist males," "sexual exploitation," "stunted potential," and "sisterhood." The rising dignity of the once downtrodden women of America was the hottest topic of conversation at every cocktail party.

The Sociology of the Movement

There seems to be little doubt that the Women's Liberation movement, at least as it is presently constituted, is, for the most part, an upper middle-class phenomena. This fact is recognized by many of the members of the movement, and the following statement by Dr. Germaine Greer (*Penthouse Magazine,* September 1971), one of the most widely quoted and according to many one of the reasonable spokesmen, clearly indicates this recognition:

> The curious thing about the female liberationists in America is that they are mostly from that class — the most privileged class of their society. And what they are doing for the women bearing the weight of the nation's economy — the housewives who do the shopping — is negligible. (p. 52)

For an understanding of this bias in the representation of the social classes within Women's Liberation one must look to the sociological origins of most of its members. In doing so, it will be possible to gain a clearer picture of the factors underlying a major fallacy of Women's Liberation — its failure to correctly analyze the adult male role in industrial society.

The majority of the advocates of Women's Liberation (both the women and their male supporters) were raised in white collar or professional environments; most of their parents lived in respectable apartments in the city or in single-family homes in the suburbs. While such environments possess many desirable comforts of life, they also possess many liabilities, one of the most serious being the narrow and sheltered character of that upbringing. Isolated from most of the everyday problems of most people, these children of the 1950s and 1960s grew up with a kind of firsthand ignorance of their own society. In America, they lacked familiarity with the way most Americans really live. Because they had been

raised in leisure, abundance, and prestige, they quite naturally assumed that all Americans lived as well as they did.
Taking this for granted, they also assumed that most people
faced the same problems that such a comfortable life style
seems to engender. Later, in high school and college, when
they turned against their parents and their upper-middle-
class, consumer-oriented life style, the young rebels made the
natural mistake of assuming that they were revolting against
the entire society. However, they were really revolting against
themselves, their own perceptions of society learned in the
sheltered and privileged segment that had spawned them. The
important question is, What characteristics of the environment gave them their weak sexual identities, caused them to
turn on their parents and the parents' life styles, and (of
importance to the Women's Liberation question) go so far
astray in their analysis of the role of most adult males in this
society?

Sociologists have determined that the essential
characteristic of upper-middle-class value systems is preoc-
cupation with a career (Kahl, 1961). By a career, the upper
middle class does not mean merely a job which one holds for
life such as machinist, truck driver, typist, or department
store clerk. These forms of employment are considered
demeaning by this class. What the upper middle class means
by career is a position with glamour, prestige, power, and
solid income potential. In addition, such positions must also
have excellent opportunity for advancement. Obviously
positions of employment that fit these characteristics are
numerically quite scarce. The short list includes corporation
executives, lawyers, physicians, college professors, and
upper-level governmental bureaucrats.

The Women's Liberationists and their brothers grew up in
homes where the central value was achievement and a career.
The career was seen as the golden gate through which one
entered the promised land of materialistic comfort, social

respect, and prestige. It was also made quite clear that careers were for men. Yet the girls in the family came to recognize the value of a career, especially when they saw that their mothers, who because they had not been forced to work outside the home like their lower-class counterparts, had little to do in their mechanized households except chauffeur children from one place to another.

There was, however, another problem. Father, the embodiment of the career, was never home; he was too busy pursuing his career to teach the children both in fact and through example what the male world and the world of careers were all about. Whenever he *was* home, he was too tired to serve as a model for anything but a man at rest, escaping reality through TV football. All the fathers in the neighborhood were also off pursuing careers. Thus, while the career was held up as the holy grail, nobody really knew much about it. It was very mysterious. Mother did not know much about it; she was merely a housewife with a lot of time on her hands — a sort of privileged class within a class. The children did not know anything about the father's career because they had so little contact with anybody who had a career.

To make matters worse, the children seldom saw or interacted with any males. Not only were fathers seldom present, but the children's teachers were almost exclusively women for the first six grades; in junior high, there were a few men: gym teachers, shop instructors, perhaps a few male history teachers. In high school there were a few more male teachers, but by this time much of the character of the boys and girls had already been set. Besides, male junior high and high school teachers make poor models for career-oriented, upper-middle-class children.

In addition, the TV programs that mother and the kids frequently watched often portrayed fathers and males in general as half-wits and stooges. "Father Knows Best,"

"Lucy," and "The Flintstones" are three examples of popular TV programs in which males are portrayed as incompetent; and the women are wily and wise. Thus, in the isolation and deprivation of the suburbs, the children of the 1950s and 1960s were raised by women. They grew up knowing little about the upper-middle-class male culture and almost nothing about male or female culture of the other social classes of society.

The effect of this deprivation of exposure to male culture is that boys and girls grew up with a distinct distaste for their mothers' lives of boredom and alienation and held a sort of idealized image of a career, which their fathers were off pursuing. With such idealization came the desire in both boys and girls to have their own careers. There were some problems in doing so, however. One of the results was a sort of collapsing of the differences in the way the sexes behaved and dressed. The boys, not having a male model to accurately imitate, became more feminine in their dress and behavior; like their mothers they grew their hair long, wore flashy clothes, and became less aggressive. The girls not wanting to be like their mothers, shunned her image and attempted to imitate features of the male model. The result was the masculinization of the pants-wearing aggressive American female. The outcome was the unisex of the upper middle class.

When these young adults graduated from high school, they went on to college and, following their studies, set out to find the valued but still little understood career. Nothing, however, breaks the bubble of fantasy faster than reality. The road to a career was much more difficult than they had supposed. The positions they desired were demanding intellectually and, consequently, often required years of specialized training.

Once attained, the career itself was far from being all gravy. The males were forced to accept their fate; the escape was to drop out, which many of them did. Many joined communes, became hippies, bums, or drug freaks. Many women dropped out also, but others stayed. They became Women's Liberationists, and cried prejudice at both real and imagined resistance to their push for more prestigious positions. By doing so, they could increase their chances of advancement. Not only would they be judged for competence, they would be judged by the white liberals from similar backgrounds. They would be evaluated by how loudly they screamed; the louder they yelled the more rapidly they would be advanced. Soon all professional halls would be filled with the caterwaller of women yodeling about sexism and job discrimination.

The Demands

Study after study conducted by women showed that there were more men than women in prestigious positions where decisions were made and power was held. The women demanded equal representation in such positions. Qualifications were largely irrelevant—they demanded quotas. If a woman was present, it was assumed that she was qualified. If men outnumbered women on prestigious jobs, it was assumed to be *prima facie* evidence of sexual discrimination. Some colleges and universities were under heavy pressure to hire only blacks, browns, and women until equality and balance had been achieved. Reverse discrimination was clearly in effect.

On university campuses, the fountainhead of both liberalism and Women's Liberation, there was widespread effort to offer courses in Women's Liberation; some women even demanded that departments be set up to offer majors in "Women's Studies." These departments were to be staffed only by women.

Insofar as the best jobs in society were concerned, women were definitely on the move. But what about the less desirable jobs in society? What of the dirty jobs, the back-breaking jobs, the jobs that ruin a worker's health, the jobs that make a worker old before his years? On this point the Women's Liberationists have been curiously silent. Like so many groups with rising expectations today, the Women's Liberationists demand equal representation on the most desirable jobs in society, but nothing is said of the routine jobs which must also be done. Is it to be assumed that men should continue to occupy the bloody job of war? (And anybody who thinks we are not going to have any more wars doesn't know his history or his anthropology; see Newcomb, 1950, 1960 for a most insightful discussion of the causes of war.) Is it to be assumed that men should continue to drive the big diesel trucks and operate the heavy earth-moving equipment, both of which shake loose and reduce the efficiency of the kidneys? Is it to be assumed that men should continue to do all the dreary, meaningless jobs in the construction industry: laborer, carpenter, etc? Is it to be assumed that men should continue to descend into the earth to dig coal and minerals and in the process have their lungs progressively filled with coal and other rock dust? As one tough old Nevada miner said recently, "I never saw one of them digging in a piss ditch in a tunnel." (A piss ditch in a tunnel is a drainage ditch in a mine whose maintenance is considered physically one of the most demanding jobs where all jobs are difficult. The floor of the tunnel is usually solid rock and the air is bad, filled with diesel exhaust and powder gas from blasting. The least exertion obviously necessary to dig in the rock produces a roaring headache as well as extreme fatigue.)

Since the Women's Liberationists are so conspicuously silent on the equal distribution of the real dirty jobs, we can only assume that they will try to avoid such jobs if possible. It is more likely that the upper middle-class chauvinists may be generous and bequeath to the lower-class women all the undesirable jobs which they have no intention of taking. They themselves will commandeer the cream of occupations. It is interesting to note that, at least in the Western states, women replaced men in one of the traditionally male jobs in the road construction industry. On many road building projects, it is now quite common to see women serving as "flagmen," directing traffic around construction sites. The only problem is that this has traditionally been considered one of the easiest jobs on a road building project, having usually been reserved for elderly men, sick men who needed money, or men who had been injured on other more demanding activities on the project.

What Women's Liberationists and their supporters have assumed is that all jobs have the same meaning, dignity, and income potential as the professional positions to which they aspire. Their social backgrounds account for this misunderstanding, but it could not be further from the truth. Most jobs consist of drudgery; there is little meaning and dignity involved except as a means of keeping food on the table. Most jobs do not afford the prestige and flexible hours that professional positions do. Neither do they afford the opportunities for decision-making or exercising one's creativity. Most jobs are boring, and the real problem is not finding a more equitable distribution of jobs among the sexes or the races. The problem is eliminating as many of the undesirable jobs as possible. The Women's Liberationists are angry, frustrated, upper-middle-class women and men who have lived sheltered lives in suburban homes and high-rise apartments, and who know even less about the problems of most people than they do about the sources of their own frustrations.

2

Complaints Many and Various
—Graves

While I support some of the demands of the Women's Liberation movement (for example, equal pay for equal jobs, abortion on demand, and day care centers for working mothers), I must take exception to the movement's attack on some of the most basic aspects of our society: the nuclear family, male domination, and the division of labor.

The Attack on the Family

A survey of Women's Liberation literature reveals several dominant themes including male hostility, domination, exploitation, and advocation of homosexuality in one form or another. However, no complaint seems more important or central to the logic of the Women's Liberationists' arguments than the almost universal hostility toward the institution of the human nuclear family. Most of the leading writers in the movement tend, in one way or another, to blame the family for virtually all their woes. Several quotations will illustrate this point. Kate Millett (1971), one of the most militant and widely quoted of the Women's Liberationists, commented on the patriarchal organization of society:

> If one takes patriarchal government to be the institution whereby that half of the populace which is female is controlled by the half which is male, the principles of

patriarchy appear to be two fold: male shall dominate female, elder male shall dominate younger. . . . (p. 25) Patriarchy's chief institution is the family. It is both a mirror of and a connection with the larger society; a patriarchal unit within a patriarchal whole. Mediating between the individual and the social structure, the family effects control and conformity where political and other authorities are insufficient. As the fundamental instrument and foundation unit of patriarchal society the family and its roles are prototypical. Serving as an agent of the larger society, the family not only encourages its own members to adjust and conform, but acts as a unit in the government of the patriarchal state which rules its citizens through its family heads. Even in patriarchal societies where they are granted legal citizenship, women tend to be ruled through the family alone and have little or no formal relation to the state. . . (p. 33)

We are not accustomed to associate patriarchy with force. So perfect is its system of socialization, so complete the general assent to its values, so long and so universally has it prevailed in human society, that it scarcely seems to require violent implementation. . . (p. 43) A sexual revolution would require, perhaps first of all, an end of traditional sexual inhibitions and taboos, particularly those that most threaten patriarchal monogamous marriage: homosexuality, "illegitimacy," adolescent, pre- and extra-marital sexuality . . . a sexual revolution would bring the institution of patriarchy to an end, abolishing both the ideology of male supremacy and the traditional socialization by which it is upheld in matters of status, role, and temperament. This would produce an integration of the separate sexual subcultures, and assimilation by both sides of previously segregated human experience. (p. 62)

In her discussion of the "sexual revolution" Millett leans heavily on the work of the nineteenth century social philosopher Frederich Engels. Such a reliance, I believe, reveals another common and essential theme of Women's Liberation. The liberated women show a pronounced penchant for "communal" social arrangement. First Millett quotes Engels: "With the transformation of the means of production into collective property, the monogamous family will cease to be the economic unit of society. The care and education of children becomes a public matter." In her comment on Engels' remark, Millet clearly reveals her attitude toward the family and to one of its most important functions: child rearing.

> This last point, is perhaps the most crucial of Engels' propositions, though it meets with the greatest resistance. There is something logical and even inevitable in this recommendation, for as long as every female, simply by virtue of her anatomy, is obliged, even forced, to be the sole or primary caretaker of childhood, she is prevented from being a free human being. The care of children, even from the period when their cognitive powers first emerge, is infinitely better left to the best trained practitioners of both sexes who have chosen it as a vocation, rather than to harried and all too frequently unhappy persons with little time nor taste for the work of educating minds, however young or beloved. The radical outcome of Engels' analysis is that the family, as that term is presently understood, must go. In view of the institution's history, this is a kind fate. (pp. 126-127)

In the introduction to a volume of essays that she edited, Robin Morgan (1970) is equally hostile toward the family.

> One thing does seem clearer as time goes on: The nuclear family unit is oppressive to women (*and* children, *and* men). The woman is forced into a totally dependent position, paying for her keep with an enormous amount of emotional and physical labor which is not even considered work. . .In essence women are still back in feudal times. We work outside capitalism, as unpaid labor—and it is the structure of the family that makes this possible, since the employer pays only the husband and, in fact, gets the rest of the family's services for free. (p. xxxii)

In an article in Morgan's volume, Dr. Mary Jane Sherfey also has harsh words for the human family. In addition, she seems to blame all of civilized history for the subjugation of women and the ruthless repression of the human female's alleged tremendous sex drive. While the theory is interesting it is without scientific merit.

> Many factors have been advanced to explain the rise of the patriarchal, usually polygamous, system and its concomitant ruthless subjugation of female sexuality (which necessarily subjugated her entire emotional and intellectual life). However, if the conclusions reached here are true, it is conceivable that forceful suppression of woman's inordinate sexual demands was a prerequisite to the dawn of every modern civilization and almost every living culture. Primitive woman's sexual drive was too strong, too susceptible to the fluctuating extremes of an impelling, aggressive erotism to withstand the disciplined requirements of a settled family life—where many living children were necessary to a family's well-being and where paternity had become as important as maternity in maintaining family and property cohesion. . .
>
> There are many indications from the prehistory studies in the Near East that it took perhaps five thousand years or longer for the subjugation of women to take place. All relevant data from the 12,000 to 8,000 B.C. period indicate that precivilized woman enjoyed full sexual freedom and was often totally incapable of controlling her sexual drive. Therefore, I propose that one of the reasons for the long delay between the earliest development of agriculture (c. 12,000 B.C.) and the rise of urban life and the beginning of recorded knowledge (c. 8,000-5,000 B.C.) was the ungovernable cyclic sexual drive of women. (Morgan, 1970, pp. 223-225)

Martha Shelly, a "radical lesbian," does not mention the family directly, but quite explicitly makes her views known regarding many of the social activities that constitute an important part of family life.

Lesbianism is one road to freedom—freedom from oppression by men . . . The Lesbian, through her ability to obtain love and sexual satisfaction from another woman, is freed of dependence on men for love, sex, and money. She does not have to do menial chores for them (at least at home), nor cater to their egos, nor submit to hasty and inept sexual encounters. She is freed from fear of unwanted pregnancy and pains of childbirth, and from the drudgery of child raising. (Morgan, 1970, pp. 306-307)

Like Millett, Karen Sacks also views the family from the perspective of Marxist philosophy.

It is necessary to look a little more closely at the relationship of the man-woman conflict within working-class family structure to the class conflict of capitalist society. In the family, production and consumption come together. The wage earner produces the capitalists' profit and his or her family realizes this profit through consumption. For the capitalist, a society made up of a lot of nuclear families is a joy . . . A woman's childraising responsibilities are the excuse given by the capitalists for assigning women to a superexploited position. Since infants and children are economically unproductive, the capitalists see no reason to have day-care centers; they cost money. (Morgan, 1970, pp. 462-464)

Even Germaine Greer minces no words when it comes to the institution of the family. (*Playboy*, January 1972, p. 72)

I'm passionately opposed to the nuclear family, with its mom and dad and their 2.4 children, I think it's the most neurotic life style ever developed. There's just no space between the mother and the children. And the husband, on the other hand, is an extraneous element in the household who usually just exacerbates the tension that already exists between the mother and the child. The nuclear family's just too small, too introspective and incestuous a unit.

When asked if a good marriage would be a test of how liberated a woman can be, Gloria Steinem replied, "As for my marrying—no. Not until marriage laws change. Because marriage itself, or marriage and the family, are now instruments of women's oppression." (Interview, *Redbook Magazine*, January, 1972)

Sociologist Dr. Alice S. Rossi has summed up the Women's Liberation attitude:

> Some of the views of the radical feminists are just a put-down of working-class life. They are the views of women who believe their educations and refined tastes allow them to look down their noses at the skills that go into making a nest, a home, with some taste and love. (*Psychology Today*, August 1972, p. 72).

With these comments in mind we can now examine some general principles of behavior and evolution and the specific role the evolution of the family has played in the development of differences in behavioral predispositions between men and women. By doing so it may be possible to see where the Women's Liberationists have gone wrong in their thinking regarding the family.

Behavior and Evolution

Darwin established over a century ago that the survival of an organism was dependent on its biological traits. Those individuals whose traits were best adapted to an environment, he noted, survived and lived to reproduce their kind, while those less well adapted perished, failing to reproduce. It is now well recognized that the effect of such selective processes over many generations is to give rise to living forms supremely adapted to their environments. This principle has been shown to be true for the lowest microbe as well as man. (Since environments are continually changing, selection for adaptation to those environments is also continuous. Thus, the process of adaptation of a species is never ending.)

During the last one hundred ten years evolutionists have been able to demonstrate how tens of thousands of physical traits in hundreds of species of organisms are important to the survival of the bearers of those traits. It has only been during the last decade, or so, however, that scientists have become acutely aware that the *behavior* of the organism is also important is the selection of who lives to reproduce and who does not. It matters little whether an animal possesses a well adapted skeleton, digestion, and circulation if its behavior is such that it is prone to get itself eaten by another animal. In some environments, for instance, an excess of curiosity can be more deadly than faulty digestion.

Much, if not most, of an organism's behavior is dependent upon the characteristics of its physical body, with the traits of the nervous system among the most important. In addition to being responsible for regulating basic body functions, such as respiration, blood circulation, and temperature, the nervous system in higher animals is, largely through the actions of the brain, also responsible for the organization and execution of behavior. The brain is the organ that gives the orders to eat, drink, sleep, engage in sex, play, laugh, run, fight, get angry, and kill. If an organism's nervous system is so constructed that it predisposes its owner to engage in behavior that makes survival possible, then in all likelihood the characteristics of that nervous system will be passed on to the offspring. If, on the other hand, the nervous system is so constructed as to predispose its owner to engage in behavior that gets him killed, then obviously the owner will do little or no reproducing. Thus, in any species of animal, including man, there is a constant selective pressure for nervous systems as well as bodies that are able to initiate and execute adaptive life-preserving behavior.

The converse of this point is important for the following discussion. Since in evolution there is a dynamic interplay between behavior and the physical traits that make possible the behavior in the first place, the adoption of adaptive behavior by an organism leads to selective favoring of the physical traits that initiate and facilitate that behavior. *Put more simply, over time and many generations adaptive behavior of an organism leads to biological change; the biological change then predisposes the organism to that behavior.* Perhaps an illustration will help to clarify this principle.

Some of the best records in the study of genetics and evolution are obtained from experiments with fruit flies. In addition to being inexpensive to maintain in large colonies, fruit flies can produce many generations in a single year, allowing the investigator to study evolution in microcosm, as it were. In a recent experiment (Tinbergen, 1971) two strains of fruit flies were selected for a study of behavior. (Dobzhansky (1972) has a report of a similar experiment.) Equal numbers of both sexes and both strains were mixed and allowed to mate. At the beginning of the experiment it was found that the two strains interbred quite readily in the natural state, showing a slight preference for their own kind.

The equivalent of intense selective pressure was applied by killing all hybrid offspring, that is, products of cross matings. Pure offspring of both strains (products of likes mating with likes) were allowed to survive and again mixed and mated. This process was continued for three years, by which time forty generations of fruit flies had passed. At the termination of the experiments, selection against the hybrids was found to have had a marked effect on the interbreeding pattern of the two strains. Previously the two strains had interbred indiscriminately; it was now found that the males of both strains of the last generation mated preponderately with females of their own strain, and females courted by males of the other strain refused the amorous overtures more consistently than had the females of the first generation. Thus, in a mere forty generations, no more than twelve hundred years in terms of human generations, what is analogous to maladaptive behavior in fruit flies was markedly reduced through selective pressures. It would be difficult to determine what physical changes took place in the flies as a result of the experiment. However, there is no question that a physical change of some sort took place, for the focus of selection was on the genetic structure of the fruit flies and genetic structures regulate physical traits. Thus, in the fruit flies we have an example of how selection against maladaptive behavior can lead to an increase in the predisposition toward adaptive behavior ("adaptation" always defined in terms of the environment). This simplistic example concerns lower organisms, but it illustrates a principle that undoubtedly applies to man.

One further point is necessary. Among lower animals, for example, flies or birds, expression of inborn predispositions toward certain behavior tends to be independent or at least less dependent on environmental factors. Inborn proclivities toward certain behavior tend to unfold regardless of whether the behavior is appropriate. An example of such inappropriate behavior can be seen in "imprinting" in ducks. Ducklings become "attached" to and will follow for life any moving stimulus to which they are exposed during a critical period following hatching. Ordinarily the moving object is the mother duck. However, if a pinwheel is substituted for the mother at the critical time, the ducks will become attached to and follow the pinwheel for life.

Among more advanced species of animals, such as man, the unfolding of behavioral prescriptions is more dependent on environmental factors: the behaviors themselves are less stereotyped. *One measure of such behavior prescriptions is the ease with which certain behaviors are learned and the difficulty with which still other behaviors are learned.* (Hamburg, 1969) The relative ease with which children learn language is an example of the "unfolding of innate behavior." The ease with which human beings learn heterosexual behavior is another. The ease with which man learns aggression as well as cooperation are two others. All of these behaviors have had adaptive value in the past and consequently there has undoubtedly been selection for them.

Evolution of the Family

George Peter Murdock (1957), an eminent anthropologist, has described and analyzed 554 human societies from the most simple hunting and gathering societies such as the Bushmen of Africa and the Aborigines of Australia to the most advanced industrial societies such as our own. During the last one hundred years many of the simpler societies have ceased to exist; a few, however, still survive. Murdock has found that 415 of the 554 human societies (75 percent) practice legalized polygamy (one husband, many wives). One hundred eighty-one (181) practice it on a limited basis, 231 practice it generally. Murdock found general polygamy particularly prevalent in Africa, monogamy in the circum-Mediterranean (the area from which American culture is derived), limited polygamy in the Insular Pacific, and sororal polygamy (where a man takes two or more sisters for his wives) in North American Indians. Only 24 percent practice legalized monogamy. In only 4 societies, less than 1 percent, polyandry (one wife, many husbands) was the preferred form of marriage. Polyandry is practiced by the Toda of South India, the Nayar of India, and in the Marquesas of Eastern Polynesia and Tibet. Put another way, of the 419 societies that permit an individual to take more than one spouse at the same time, 415 permit a man to take more than one wife; 4 permit a woman to take more than one husband. There is wide agreement among anthropologists that statistically the polyandrous societies are insignificant, and analysis has demonstrated they occur only under extreme environmental conditions where there is a shortage of women or where one man cannot provide enough food for one woman and her children. Further, there is nothing in the anthropological record to indicate that the situation has been any different during the last half million or more years.

Also relevant to this discussion are "rules of residence"—the rules of a society that dictate where and with whose family newlyweds will live. Murdock (1957) found in that same study that of the 565 societies sampled, 376 are predominately patrilocal; that is, newlyweds are required to reside with or near the husband's family. Only 84 are predominately matrilocal, requiring newlyweds to reside with or near the bride's family.

The reckoning of an individual's descent through his mother's or father's line is also significant. Societies in which individuals trace their membership through the father's line outnumber those in which membership is traced through the mother's line four to one. Hunters and gatherers reside almost exclusively with the groom's family and nearly always trace group membership through the male side of the family (D'Andrade, 1966).

Studies of the evolution of culture suggest that prior to the domestication of plants and animals some ten thousand years ago, all peoples probably lived much as contemporary hunters and gatherers do today; that is, they foraged off the land consuming only wild plants and small and big game animals. In terms of marriage and social organization, hunting and gathering societies are almost always polygynous or monogymous.

These statistics suggest that human beings cohabit more easily in a situation of plural wives than in a situation of plural husbands. The frequency of the practice of plural wives suggests that the arrangement has some social value and, consequently, some survival value. If such an arrangement did not have some survival value, it seems unlikely that so many societies over the hundreds of thousands of years would have adopted it. Thus, in terms of the previous evolutionary arguments a strong contention can be made that human beings have an innate proclivity to reside in social arrangements comprised of one man and one wife or one man and many wives, but do not exhibit a proclivity to live in an arrangement consisting of one wife and many husbands.

37

Such an argument has strength because polygyny is assumed to have survival value, and it can be expected that behavior that has survival value will lead to physical changes which in turn predispose the individual to such behavior. If this is true, it seems likely that the need for residence in certain family arrangements is an important part of mankind's nature. The nature of the human male lies in the direction of residence with plural wives, and the nature of the human female lies in the direction of sharing one male with co-wives or residence with a single male rather than marital cohabitation with more than one male. Arrangements along any other lines appear to be contrary to the natural grain of man's innate behavioral tendencies.

This point becomes even more evident when one examines what seems to be the origin of the human family. Of all the mammals, the human female and the rabbit are among the few who do not need to be in estrus (ovulating) to be sexually receptive to the male. Unlike the female rabbit, who ovulates following coitus, the human female, like the majority of mammals, ovulates cyclically. That is to say, the human female is in theory always sexually receptive but is periodically fertile. Why does the human female possess these unique behavioral and reproductive traits?

In the animal kingdom, the primates are man's closest relatives. In fact, man himself is classified as a primate. In addition to man, all monkeys and apes are members of this group. Primates are mammals and have many traits in common, including keen vision, the grasping hand, and a highly developed brain. These common traits suggest a relatively recent common origin (less than 70 million years) on an immense evolutionary time scale.

An examination of primate behavior and the drawing of a few inferences concerning the possible evolution of human behavior and social organization suggest some answers. Among the primates the gibbon, an ape from southeast Asia

who dwells almost exclusively in trees, is the only ape known
to be monogymous. The remainder of the primates, particularly the ground-dwelling species, reside in variably sized
groups sometimes called troops. Within the troops, the
biggest and most dominant males are in command; they serve
as group leaders and settle internal squabbles and fights
between subdominant group members. They also serve as
group defenders, and among the larger species, such as man's
ancestors must have been, dominant males can be quite
vicious when threatened and have been known to attack
outright even the largest of predators (Eisenberg, 1972).
Although there is variability among different species of
primates, a female in estrus (heat) will sometimes mate with
subdominant males. More often matings are confined exclusively to dominant males, or matings with dominant
males take place when conception is most likely to occur
while matings with subdominant males take place when
conception is unlikely. In most species of primates, the lives
of adult females are dominated by infant care (Eisenberg,
1972). Males are tolerant and protective toward the young
but participate minimally in such activities. Thus, while a
primate group might be composed of a large number of
variably aged and sexed individuals, the subhuman primate
"family" remains a sort of primeval matriarchy consisting of
the mother and infant diad, with each mother being primarily
responsible for her own infant. Since the females are not
continuously receptive to the sexual needs of the males, the
males dominate and otherwise service only females who are
in estrus and only those who will have them. There is reason
to suppose that as much as several million years ago man's
ancestors organized their societies in such a manner, that is a
primitive matriarchy consisting of females and infants and a
sort of primitive if highly limited and restrictive promiscuity
in sexual activity.

As such a society became more advanced and complex,
however, and as the members, through evolution, grew more

intelligent, their behavioral repertoire increased; the deficiencies of this system of social organization became more evident. Two essential factors were involved in the increased inefficiency. Since there was no recognition of social or physiological paternity, males probably did not assist much in the care of infants. As a consequence there was little division of labor within the biological family unit. Females were in effect forced to do most of the work in caring for the young. Since the period of infantile dependence must have been increasing as a result of increased intelligence and social complexity, this burden must have been considerable. In addition, promiscuous behavior on the part of males and females and inequitable access of subdominant males to females must have been highly disruptive socially.

It seems probable that these two serious social problems that our ancestors faced were solved with one rather simple evolutionary adjustment. Our female ancestors, instead of being sexually receptive on a periodic basis, developed continuous sexual receptivity. Continuous sexual receptivity had the effect of creating a more equitable distribution of sex among all males in the group regardless of their position in the dominance hierarchy. More equitable distribution of sex led to the development of a stable male-female diad—the relationship that is the basis of the human family everywhere in the world. A shift from the mother-child diad, and the development of a stable male-female diad led to the involvement of the male in the raising of the young. This division of labor made it more probable that the young would survive in the increasingly complex social order. This formed the basis for the selection of the trait of continuous female sexual receptivity. Continuous sexual receptivity of the female led to a reduction in social disruption by providing a sexual outlet for all adult males of the society. Involvement of males in the care of the young probably also reduced social disruptions through increased social integration of subdominant males.

Integration of subdominant males into the mainstream of social life led to the availability of a greater number of males for defense duties and eventually to armed conflict and systematic efforts at territorial expansion and defense.

It was in such a manner that both males and females were "programmed" by evolution for their sex and work roles within what we now know as the human family. The individual's drive to reside within some sort of traditional family arrangement probably has much the same biological basis as the need to express oneself through language.

It is on this essential fact, perhaps more than any other, that the Women's Liberationists have gone astray. To many this point may seem to be little more than obvious but it, as well as its logic, is important. The human nuclear family is the foundation of all but a very few societies and attacks upon it can only be misplaced and dangerous.

It is not the family that is the archenemy of women. Quite the contrary. It seems more probably that it is within the historical confines of the nuclear (and extended) family, that both female and male best satisfy a myriad of uniquely human yet ancient needs. For hundreds of thousands of years selective pressures have favored men and women who live in families. Throughout much of history life outside the family was tantamount to nothing short of death itself. In the next few decades technologically based cultural forces may make family living extremely difficult. But this has nothing to do with the needs evolution has programmed into man's nervous system.

A new society characterized by communes, group sex, and state care of children is nothing short of nonsense, especially for Americans who have a long tradition of independence and individualism. No society in which group sex was practiced has survived for an extended period of time. In those few societies, such as the Reindeer Chukchee of Siberia, where group sex was ostensibly practiced, sexual rights to another's mate were seldom exercised. Societies organized on the basis of extreme promiscuity are short-lived—extreme promiscuity inevitably leads to social disruption. Men and women are basically possessive of their mates. The expression of modest amounts of jealousy and concern when one's rights to one's mate are realistically threatened is not a sign of emotional immaturity, which many of the more normless members of the avantgarde would have us believe. The legitimate expression of jealousy is a basic and healthy emotional experience. It is emotional preparation for action, designed for the protection of one's self-interest. After all, what could be more germane to one's self-interest than action calculated to protect the love and life that one has built with a member of the opposite sex?

The contention that the state should raise children is equally untenable. Again, most women have been programmed by evolution to need children and to need to care for them. Among the majority of mammals, the most rigorous kind of selective pressure has favored this trait. A mother who does not properly care for her offspring soon loses them to accident and predators, and consequently, does not pass her nonchalance on to the next generation. A woman who cannot live with a man and bear and raise children in efficiency and a degree of harmony does not have many children survive and consequently does not pass on her incompatibilities insofar as they are biologically based, and all behavioral traits possess a biological component.

As with so many behavioral traits in man, it appears that much behavior associated with motherhood is to an extent regulated by hormones. One example is the pituitary hormone prolactin, which, in addition to causing milk secretion in nursing women, is believed by many researchers to be related to the mother's love or acceptance of the child.

The Attack on Male Domination

Male "domination" over females has been one of the most heatedly discussed aspects of the Women's Liberation movement. Experimentation and observation of primates indicate that male domination is both natural and desirable.

Among natural ranging primates males are always dominant over females. Recent experiments conducted at the Yerkes Regional Primate Center in Atlanta, Georgia, indicate that male monkeys have a strong tendency to dominate female monkeys (*Science News*, April 29, 1972). Among rhesus monkeys testosterone levels (male hormones) correlate somewhat with social dominance and aggressive behavior. (This will be discussed further in the next chapters.) To determine how levels of testosterone were affected by social factors among rhesus monkeys, researchers measured the testosterone levels of four adult males who had been caged separately, and then placed each in a compound with three females for two weeks. The males were then returned to their own cages for two weeks and then placed for fifteen- to thirty-minute intervals in a compound with a well-established group of thirty adult males. Afterward they were returned to their own pens and at a later date reintroduced into the female compound.

The effect on the testosterone levels of the four males and their behavior was quite dramatic. When housed with the females, the experimental males quickly achieved a dominant status and were sexually active. Testosterone levels increased an average of 183 percent. Following the monkeys' removal from the female compound, hormone levels returned to normal within two weeks. When the males were introduced into the male group, however, they were attacked; hormone levels fell by 80 percent and remained low for up to 60 days after removal from the male cage. When the males were reintroduced into the female group, their hormone levels again rose as they reassumed the dominant role.

Every investigation of subhuman primate groups has shown males dominant over females. In primate societies, dominant males tend to lead subdominant males and females tend to follow. A system of male-leader, female-follower probably leads to greater group cohesion, makes group defense easier, and hence facilitates the survival of all group members.

Such a system of leadership and authority has survival value, and behavior that has survival value eventually leads to appropriate physical changes that predispose future generations to that behavior. Thus, it seems reasonable to argue that the female primate is predisposed to be submissive to the male.

Further, despite the wide range in forms of human societies, nowhere, not even in the matriarchies, are women really dominant. In all cases and in all known societies, men make the majority of the most important decisions and women in one degree or another are submissive to men. Some scholars argue and equivocate on this point, contending that in a few societies, admittedly numerically insignificant, women are equal in dominance to men. If this is true, and there is much evidence to suggest that it is not, such societies are, in terms of evolutionary time, quite recent developments. The truth is that human beings have lived all but the last few thousand years in hunting and gathering societies and evidence suggests that such societies were probably always male-oriented, at least since the origin of the male-female diad family. Anthropologists believe that male orientation in hunting and gathering groups is derived from the social values of the males' protection of the group as well as the long period of time needed for a man to learn to effectively hunt in a given area (Service, 1972). A consequence of this can be seen in the fact that in such societies women almost always leave their own group at marriage and go to reside in their husband's group; the relationship of the children of that union is usually reckoned through the father's family and not through the mother's. Thus, it seems likely that throughout most of human history the dominance of women by men has been a vital fact of life and that this situation has given rise to a propensity, a need, for the female to be to some degree or another dominated by and submissive to the male. Consequently it seems likely that it is in such a relationship that both the male and the female find true expression of their "inbuilt" nature. Naturally, as with all innate traits, there probably exists a range, with some women requiring a good deal of domination, while other women require little or no domination and may even prefer to dominate. The reverse is undoubtedly also true for males; some need to be quite aggressive and dominating, while others prefer to be dominated. Taken as two groups, however, it is probable that women require some external domination from the male for maximum contentment and self-fulfillment while men require a female to dominate and protect for maximum self-actualization. This is not to say that women are somehow inferior to men or deficient; but they are different. Those differences are attributable, in the final analysis, to the operation of evolutionary forces.

The Attack on the Division of Labor

The broadest attack the movement makes on our society is on the traditional division of labor. Let us examine this practice, its prevalence and practicality.

All societies practice division of labor. As noted in Chapter 1, one of the primary means that societies have devised for dividing up the labor is along the lines of sex. Males are assigned certain tasks; females are assigned others. One of the interesting things about the way in which societies divide the labor between the sexes is that cultures around the world tend consistently to assign the same tasks to men and women. In one study (Murdock, 1935) of the sex-based division of labor in 224 societies it was found that males

45

appeared to be assigned tasks requiring strength, cooperation, mobility, and long periods of travel. Female activities,
on the other hand, were found to involve less physical strain,
more solidarity, and less mobility. (See Tables 1 and 2.) It has
been noted (Dornbusch, 1966) that hunting and gathering
societies show greater sexual differentiation in task assignment than other types of societies. In hunting and gathering
societies men are primarily responsible for hunting, warfare,
and religious duties while women are responsible for child
care and the collection of vegetable foods. In general the
duties of the men take them away from the encampment
while the duties of the females tend to keep them close to the
camp.

Several explanations have been offered for these rather
consistent findings. One school of thought suggests that
differences in task assignment are based on what is called
sexual dimorphism; the male of the species possess greater
size and strength and is physically more suited to strenuous
tasks. Since this only explains the assignment of a small
percentage of the duties, the theory goes on to suggest that
once tasks involving greater strength and ability have been
assigned to males, closely related duties that do not necessarily require these traits are also assigned to males. An example
of a male task is warfare, and the associated, almost
exclusively male task is the production of weapons for war.
Women, it is argued, could make weapons but this duty is
closely associated psychologically with male war-making
activities. Duties such as child care and food gathering are
assigned to women because they involve less strength; food
preparation is closely associated with the collection of the
foods. Another similar theory for the division of labor holds
that women, who are frequently being burdened with
pregnancy, breast-feeding, and child care, are assigned jobs
that involve less mobility. While these explanations for the
traditional division of labor in societies are certainly valid,
they in fact constitute only a partial explanation. They tend

Table 1

*Cross-Cultural Data from 224 Societies on Subsistence
Activities and Division of Labor by Sex*

| Activity | Number of Societies in Which Activity is Performed by | | | | |
	Men always	Men usually	Either sex	Women usually	Women always
Pursuit of sea mammals	34	1	0	0	0
Hunting	166	13	0	0	0
Trapping small animals	128	13	4	1	2
Herding	38	8	4	0	5
Fishing	98	34	19	3	4
Clearing land for agriculture	73	22	17	5	13
Dairy operations	17	4	3	1	13
Preparing and planting soil	31	23	33	20	37
Erecting and dismantling shelter	14	2	5	6	22
Tending fowl and small animals	21	4	8	1	39
Tending and harvesting crops	10	15	35	39	44
Gathering shellfish	9	4	8	7	25
Making and tending fires	18	6	25	22	62
Bearing burdens	12	6	35	20	57
Gathering fruits, berries, nuts	12	3	15	13	63
Gathering fuel	22	1	10	19	89
Preservation of meat and fish	8	2	10	14	74
Gathering herbs, roots, seeds	8	1	11	7	74
Cooking	5	1	9	28	158
Carrying water	7	0	5	7	119
Grinding grain	2	4	5	13	114

Source: Adapted from Murdock (1935) in Roy G. D'Andrade, "Sex Differences and Cultural Institutions," in *The Development of Sex Differences,* Eleanor E. Maccoby, ed. (Stanford University Press, Stanford, Calif.), 1966.

Table 2

*Cross-Cultural Data on the Manufacture of Objects and
Division of Labor by Sex*

Activity	Number of Societies in Which Activity is Performed by				
	Men always	Men usually	Either sex	Women usually	Women always
Metalworking	78	0	0	0	0
Weapon making	121	1	0	0	0
Boat building	91	4	4	0	1
Manufacture of musical instruments	45	2	0	0	1
Work in wood and bark	113	9	5	1	1
Work in stone	68	3	2	0	2
Work in bone, horn, shell	67	4	3	0	3
Manufacture of ceremonial objects	37	1	13	0	1
House building	86	32	25	3	14
Net making	44	6	4	2	11
Manufacture of ornaments	24	3	40	6	18
Manufacture of leather products	29	3	9	3	32
Hide preparation	31	2	4	4	49
Manufacture of nontextile fabrics	14	0	9	2	32
Manufacture of thread and cordage	23	2	11	10	73
Basket making	25	3	10	6	82
Mat making	16	2	6	4	61
Weaving	19	2	2	6	67
Pottery making	13	2	6	8	77
Manufacture and repair of clothing	12	3	8	9	95

Source: Adapted from Murdock (1935) in Roy G. D'Andrade, "Sex Differences and Cultural Institutions," in *The Development of Sex Differences,* Eleanor E. Maccoby, ed. (Stanford University Press, Stanford, Calif.), 1966.

to give only a functional explanation for behavior at a given point in time. They say in effect that because women have children and men are stronger it is convenient for the society to divide up the labor in the manner in which it does. The one thing that the study of cultures has demonstrated, however, is that convenience is not necessarily the wellspring of behavior.

Evolution of the Division of Labor

If the division of labor is viewed from the perspective of human evolution, say tens of thousands of generations in which our ancestors lived as hunters and gatherers, then the inadequacy of these functional explanations becomes more evident. In seeking a more complete explanation one must ask from an evolutionary perspective how sexual dimorphism is related to traditional patterns of division of labor. One prominent anthropologist, Dr. Roy C. D'An-drade (1966) has suggested that "some of the present biological sex differences . . . may be due to selective factors operating as a result of cultural universals in the division of labor." In this statement Dr. D'Andrade is suggesting, for example, that hunters and gatherers divide the labor of their society not only because of convenience but because through selection evolutionary forces have given rise to sexual differences which in turn make traditional ways of dividing up the labor more convenient. With time, natural selection reinforces traditional behavior. Thus not only do men hunt because they are bigger, but hunting "selects" for bigger individuals. Men go to war not only because they are bigger and faster than women, but also because warfare and social survival select for bigger and faster men. At the same time, it must be emphasized that there is undoubtedly selection for the appropriate mental and psychological predispositions to hunting and warfare behavior.

Using this mode of thought it is possible to speculate on some differences in mental traits between men and women;

these traits can be traced to selective forces acting on ancient patterns of division of labor.

Women of hunting and gathering societies were probably faced with very practical, immediate, and down-to-earth problems. These problems centered around child care, camp maintenance, and the gathering and preparation of food. It seems likely that their decisions, involving a minimum of speculation, dealt mainly with objects in the immediate material environment. Men of the same society must have faced problems of a different nature. Perhaps they were more abstract and speculative, pertaining to war and the hunt. In addition, since men were primarily responsible for religious practice, much of a male's mental activity must have dealt with the theoretical structure of the religion and the other worldly forms of spirits, gods, ancestors, and real and supposed enemies. Perhaps selection was operative here to provide women with minds that were more practical and men with minds that were more at home with the macroscopic, speculative, and theoretical concerns.

This theory receives some confirmation in the fact that most of the world's great science, art, music and literature has been produced by men. Sexual discrimination is the usual explanation for woman's poor showing. No doubt this is an important factor; but is it the only one? I have taught at a number of colleges and universities and have read widely in a variety of scientific disciplines. During this time I have encountered only a few women who possess what I would classify as first-class scientific or theoretical minds. This would apply to colleagues as well as students. On the other hand, I have frequently been impressed by the ability of many women to make sound decisions, and I have constantly been impressed with the seemingly ubiquitous ability among males to go off on a tangent, chase rainbows, and frequently make abominably bad practical decisions. A lawyer who frequently represents women in divorce cases in the United

States recently commented that he has become very much aware of the good judgment which most women exercise in the divorce proceedings and how remarkably resourceful many of them are when it comes to the everyday decisions which affect their lives. The lawyer noted that it appeared to him that women frequently appeared to exercise better judgment and greater resourcefulness than the men they were divorcing.

If this analysis is correct it might follow that western culture may have repressed and stripped women of much of the ability to solve practical problems. It is certainly true that in other cultures women are responsible for a sphere of social and domestic life in which their authority is unquestionable. Men may dominate that society as a whole but man's authority carries little weight in the area in which the female is supreme. Western culture, especially American (for some unknown reason but one that probably relates to technology), has pictured women as fools and incompetents, incapable of making any sort of decision. Jokes about dumb blondes and wives who bankrupt their husbands by spending foolishly on trivia are two examples. Obviously our society would be much better off if woman's practical nature were allowed to surface.

We can explore another possible difference between men and women which is attributable to selection produced by ancient social practices. Among ground dwellers, and even in some species of tree-dwelling primates, the males are most concerned with defense of territory. Human society shows the same characteristics; men are usually responsible for defense of hearth and home. Historically, land has been the basis of wealth and survival. A group unable to defend its territory soon finds itself exterminated or pushed further and further into marginal environments where survival is more difficult. In the evolution of subhuman primates and modern man there probably was selection in both sexes (but especially males) for physical traits that predispose an individual to the defense of his territory. For humans, a definition of territory can sometimes be quite vague and thus defense is not well defined. When conceptions of territory become clearcut, however, defensive responses are likewise well defined. Social conceptions of territory may vary, but the basic response to defend territory does not.

For the tens of thousands of years in which man resided in hunting and gathering societies there were also selective pressures that countered the territorial drive in women. Of special importance here is that fact that, in most societies but especially hunting and gathering societies, women left the territory of their own family to live in the home and territory of their husbands. Thus, it can be argued that every woman had to break her territorial ties at least once in life, and that if her ties to her original home were too strong it would interfere with her adjustment after marriage. From this fact, it could be argued that the point of environmental reference of males tends strongly toward territory and things that have subsequently become defined as territory (such as jobs), and the point of reference for females tends to be some social group in which she is a member, first that of her father and mother, later that of her husband and perhaps his family, and certainly that of her own children. Once again it seems that evolutionary theory leads straight to the idea that there is a dynamic interaction between the form and structure of a society on one hand and the biologically-based behavioral predispositions of man on the other.

From a fresh perspective, two factors can be seen as primary determinants in the traditional patterns of divisions of labor found around the world. The first is that of convenience. It is convenient and efficient for society to assign certain tasks to those individuals who are most physically suited to the tasks. The second is evolutionary. Evolution over long periods, in effect, "programs" men and women for the social roles they have traditionally occupied.

The seeming inevitability of traditional patterns of division of labor is evident from M. E. Spiro's classic study (1956) of the Israeli kibbutz.

> The social structure of the Kibbutz is responsible for a problem of . . . serious proportions—"the problem of the woman. . . ." With the exception of politics, nothing occupies so much attention in the Kibbutz. . . . It is no exaggeration to say that if Kiryat Yedidim should ever disintegrate, the "problem of the woman" will be one of the main contributing factors.
>
> In a society in which the equality of the sexes is a fundamental premise, and in which the emancipation of women is a major goal, the fact there is a "problem of the woman" requires analysis. . . . The Youth Movement from which many Kibbutz values are derived was strongly feminist in orientation. The woman in bourgeois society, it is believed, was subjected to the male and tied to her home and family. This "biological tragedy of woman" forced her into menial roles, such as house cleaning, cooking, and other domestic duties, and prevented her from taking her place beside the man in the fields, the workshop, the laboratory, and the lecture hall.
>
> In the new society all this was to be changed. The woman would be relieved of her domestic burdens by means of the various institutions of collective living, and she could then take her place as man's equal in all the activities of life. The communal dining room would free her from the burden of cooking; the communal nurseries, from the responsibilities of raising children; the small rooms, from the job of cleaning.
>
> In a formal sense, the Kibbutz has been successful in this task. . . . In spite of "emancipation" which they have experienced in the Kibbutz, there is considerable sentiment among the women . . . that they would prefer not to have been "emancipated." Almost every couple who has left the Kibbutz has done so because of the unhappiness of the woman. . . . At a town meeting devoted to the "problem of the woman," one of the most respected women in Kiryat Yedidim—the wife of a leader of the Kibbutz movement—publicly proclaimed that the Kibbutz women had not achieved what they

had originally hoped for; as for herself, after thirty years in Kiryat Yedidim she could pronounce her life a disappointment.

One source of the woman's poor morale is that many women are dissatisfied with their economic roles. . . When the vattikim [original settlers] first settled on their land, there was no sexual division of labor. Women, like men, worked in the fields and drove tractors; men, like women, worked in the kitchen and in the laundry. Men and women, it was assumed, were equal and could perform their jobs equally well. It was soon discovered; however, than men and women were not equal. For obvious biological reasons, women could not undertake many of the physical tasks of which men were capable; tractor driving, harvesting, and other heavy labor proved too difficult for them. Moreover, women were compelled at times to take temporary leave from that physical labor of which they were capable. A pregnant woman, for example, could not work too long, even in the vegetable garden, and a nursing mother had to work near the Infants House in order to be able to feed her child. Hence, as the Kibbutz grew older and the birth rate increased, more and more women were forced to leave the "productive" branches of the economy and enter its "service" branches. But as they left the "productive" branches, it was necessary that their place be filled, and they were filled with men. The result was that the women found themselves in the same jobs from which they were supposed to have been emancipated—*cooking, cleaning, laundering, teaching, caring for children,* etc.

. . . What has been substituted for the traditional routine of housekeeping . . . is more housekeeping—and a restricted and narrow kind of housekeeping at that. Instead of cooking and sewing and baking and cleaning and laundering and caring for children, the woman at Kiryat Yedidim cooks *or* sews *or* launders *or* takes care of children for eight hours a day. . . . This new housekeeping is more boring and less rewarding than the traditional type. It is small wonder, then, given this combination of low prestige, difficult working conditions, and monotony, that the chavera [female member of the Kibbutz] has found little happiness in her economic activities. (pp. 221-230)

Some may argue that the outcome of the Israeli attempt to radically alter the sexual basis of the division of labor is tragic. This attitude, however, appears to be based on the belief that men and woman are physically and mentally identical. If one believes they are, then one might look upon the failure to equalize the sexes in the kibbutz as tragic. However if one believes that there are important differences between men and women and that it is to society's advantage to utilize these differences, then the kibbutz does not appear as tragic as it does foolhardy—a foolhardy attempt to go against the grain of nature. Some may argue that as technology continues to evolve, jobs requiring strength and agility will diminish in number and cease to be of great social importance. At such a time, it might be argued, elimination of sexual division of labor in society could be expected to have greater success. There is truth in this contention. But such a belief neglects the existence of built-in predispositions to certain behaviors that evolution has programmed into the mind of man.

Is Sex Necessary?

—Thurber

It is now technically possible to reproduce without aid
of males (or, for that matter, females) and to produce
only females. We must begin immediately to do so. The
male is a biological accident: the "Y" (male) gene is an
incomplete "X" (female) gene, that is, has an incomplete
set of chromosomes. In other words, the male is an
incomplete female, a walking abortion, aborted at the
gene state. . . (p. 514) Many women will for awhile
continue to think they dig men, but as they become
accustomed to female society and as they become
absorbed in their projects, they will eventually come to
see the utter uselessness and banality of the male.
(Excerpts from Valerie Solanis, SCUM Manifesto
[Society for Cutting Up Men] as reprinted in *Sisterhood
Is Powerful*, Robin Morgan (ed.), 1970, p. 519)

Most people realize there are important differences
between boys and girls, between men and women. Insofar as
Women's Liberation is concerned, the essential question is:
What are the origins of these differences? Most Women's
Liberationists would have us believe that while very little is
known about the origins of male-female differences, most of
what we now take for granted as being "real" differences
between men and women are in fact cultural in origin. That
is to say, the differences are learned.

The following are representative quotes.

> . . . academic women are asking how much is really known about women, about the structure of the family, and about the development of "femininity" and "masculinity." Are there really any differences between sexes, and is there any conclusive research on the subject? (Janice Law Trecker, *Saturday Review,* October 16, 1971)

> Women are not capable of running their own lives and being independent of men because they've been too successfully conditioned to be dependent. (Germaine Greer, Interview, *Penthouse Magazine,* September, 1971)

> It appears that we are not soon to be enlightened as to the existence of any significant inherent differences between male and female beyond the biogenital ones we already know. Endocrinology and genetics afford no definite evidence of determining mental-emotional differences . . . Important new research not only suggests that the possibilities of innate temperamental differences seem more remote than ever, but even raises questions as to the validity and permanence of psychosexual identity. (Kate Millett, *Sexual Politics,* p. 29)

When the spokesmen for Women's Liberation do admit to the existence of innate differences, the usual contention is that they are minimal and of little physiological and psychological importance. As with most unsophisticated and fallacious theories about the world, there is a good deal of truth in this contention. One would not expect otherwise in an animal whose behavior is so heavily dependent on learning. There is also, however, a good deal more known of the so-called innate differences between men and women and the origins of these differences than the advocates of the movement acknowledge.

During the last ten years, but particularly in the last five, a good deal of experimental research has been conducted that bears directly on the problem of inborn male-female differences. It is now possible to demonstrate that males and females of the human species are not physiological, psychological, or behavioral equivalents. This is not to say that men and women are "unequal," although in some traits there are clear instances of superiority and inferiority. The point is that viewed in terms of a significant number of traits, men and women are decidedly different, and it is erroneous to view them as equivalents.

Most of this recent research deals with the effects of sex hormones—the male androgens, especially testosterone, and the female estrogens—on the central nervous system. The evidence clearly indicates that striking differences exist in certain brain structures of males and females in a variety of animal species and that these differences are strongly associated with mental functioning and behavior.

Genetic Differences Between Male and Female

At conception, all human infants have twenty-three pairs of chromosomes. Chromosomes are long strands of genetic material along which lie thousands of small structures called genes. Individual genes are the determinants of individual traits in all living organisms. Each individual receives one of each pair of chromosomes from his mother and one of each pair from his father. There are no differences between boys and girls insofar as twenty-two of the pairs of chromosomes are concerned; they are identical for either sex. Sexual characteristics are determined by what are called the sex-linked chromosomes (the twenty-third pair). This twenty-third pair is made up of two types of sex chromosomes—X and Y. A genetic female is the result of an XX pairing, having received an X from the mother and an X from the father; the male is the result of an XY pairing, having received an X from the mother and a Y from the father. In terms of contribution to the development of sexual characteristics in the offspring, the female ovum, or egg, contains only X chromosomal material; sperm from the male contains either X or Y.

Physically the X chromosome is much larger than the Y. Consequently, since females possess two Xs and males only one, females are characterized by 4 to 5 percent more genetic material than males. As far as researchers have been able to determine, (Childs, 1965) the Y, or male chromosome, is curiously inert and contains few if any genes other than those responsible for masculine development. The X chromosome, on the other hand, contains, in addition to genes responsible for sex development, a number of genes that appear to have nothing to do with masculinization or feminization. Consequently, as a result of this significant genetic disparity, Childs, writing from the Department of Pediatrics at Johns Hopkins University School of Medicine, notes that there are "undoubtedly attributes of maleness and femaleness which have nothing to do with the origin and organization of the reproductive role. (p. 800) Two obvious examples are the relative vulnerability of the male to such recessive sex-linked traits as colorblindness and hemophilia or bleeders' disease. Other less well-known genetic-based characteristics that have been linked to the differences in the number of X chromosomes which the sexes possess include vitamin D resistant rickets, glucose-6-phosphate dehydrogenase deficiency, and differences to immunological response to both bacteria and viruses.

In one study Michaels and Rogers (1971) found significant infant male-female differences in antibody levels against five types of *E. coli* bacteria as well as rubella measles virus. Female antibody levels were found to be higher than males. The contention that the X chromosome is involved in antibody production is strengthened by the fact that females with an extra X chromosome (three in all) possess antibody levels higher than normal women with two X chromosomes. Childs (1965) has suggested that such non-masculine-feminine differences may be related to the fact that more males than females die during each decade of life and that sex differences in mortality during the human life span is between 15 to 35 percent.

The Effect of Sex Hormones

Contrary to what is commonly believed, the X and Y chromosomes do not, per se, determine the development of all of the sexual characteristics of the individual. Research has demonstrated that in either sex the tissues that eventually grow into mature sexual organs are quite plastic. The form and the manner in which sexual organs eventually function is highly dependent on the type and amount of sex hormones present while the tissues are developing. In rats, who have a relatively short gestation period, males castrated during the first twenty-four hours following birth fail to develop characteristic adult male behavior. Such rats further exhibit markedly reduced growth rates similar to that of females. In addition it has been found that ovaries and vaginas can easily be transplanted into such castrated males and the transplanted organs function in a manner similar to that in normal female rats. Castration after the third day of birth, however, results in failure of such transplants to function properly. Conversely, newborn female rate injected with the male hormone testosterone shortly after birth show no signs of estrus behavior, but later as adults and during courtship exhibit typical male behavior such as darting, hopping, and ear wiggling. Such females also fail to assume the receptive position necessary for male mounting during copulation. In addition these masculinized females are uniformly aggressive and repulsive toward males in general and frequently engage in exaggerated male behavior such as increased nosing of male genital area and mounting of males with vigorous pelvic thrusts. Again injection of females with male hormones some days after birth (twenty) results in a failure to yield such results (Harris, 1964; Martini, 1969).

Similar experiments have been repeated on guinea pigs. Like primates, guinea pigs have a relatively long gestation period; but unlike the rats, if the experiments are performed following birth, no development of the behavioral abnormalities is found. But if hormones are injected prenatally, that is, before birth, male hormones in female fetuses lead to masculinization of the external genitalia, loss of characteristic female response, and an intensification of behavior characteristic of males. If female hormones are injected into males there is no effect. However, if antagonists to male hormones are injected into male fetuses, feminization similar to that in rats results (Goy, 1968).

It may be rightly argued that experiments dealing with rat physiology and behavior have limited application to human behavior. To determine whether or not there was a continuity in the development of such behavioral abnormalities between rodents and primates, Dr. Robert W. Goy (1968), Chairman of the Department of Reproductive Physiology and Behavior at Oregon Regional Primate Center, a pioneer in research of this kind, conducted similar studies on rhesus monkeys. Monkeys were used because they are relatively inexpensive and make good laboratory research subjects—more importantly, on an evolutionary scale, rhesus monkeys are relatively close to man and their reproductive biology has strong similarities to man. Rhesus monkeys are so similar to man, in fact, that the details of ovulation in the human female were first worked out on rhesus monkeys. Dr. Goy began his experiments with the work of Dr. L. Rosenblum in mind. In his dissertation at the University of Wisconsin, Dr. Rosenblum (1961) observed striking differences between the play behavior of young male and young female monkeys. Males, Dr. Rosenblum found, engaged in significantly more "rough and tumble play" and aggression than females. Dr. Goy's technique involved isolation of newborn infant and mother for the first three and one-half months of the infant's life, whereupon the infant was weaned and individually housed. Later infants were brought together in groups of four to six individuals once a week for periods of twenty to thirty minutes. At such time the behavior of all members of the group was observed for predetermined periods of time. Such observations were continued for fifteen weeks during the first year of life and repeated for about seven weeks during the second year. Dr. Goy's findings were similar to those of Dr. Rosenblum. Striking sexual dimorphism in behavior was found to exist between the sexes. Males were found to engage significantly more in "frequency of threat," "play initiation," "rough and tumble play," and "chasing play." (See Figs. 1-4.) Such behavior, it was found, could not be attributed to the presence of the male sex hormones in the young males for repeated blood samples failed to reveal measurable amounts. Further, little difference in behavior was found between males castrated at birth and intact males.

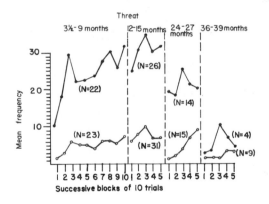

Figure 1.   Frequency of threat for normal male (● - ●) and female (o - o) rhesus monkeys during the first 3¼ years of life.

Source: E. Peretz, R.W. Goy, C.H. Phoenix, and J.A. Resko, "Influence of Gonadal Hormones on the Development and Activation of the Nervous System of the Rhesus Monkey," in *Influence of Hormones on the Nervous System*, D.H. Ford, ed. (S. Karger, New York, 1971), pp. 404—405, 408.

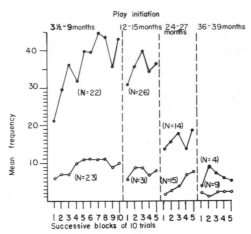

Figure 2. Frequency of play initiation for normal male (● - ●) and female (o - o) rhesus monkeys during the first 3 ¼ years of life.

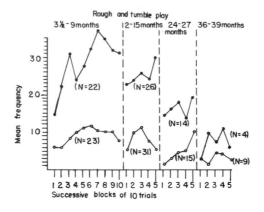

Figure 3.   Frequency of rough and tumble play for normal male (● - ●) and female (o - o) rhesus monkeys during the first 3 ¼ years of life.

Source: E. Peretz, R.W. Goy, C.H. Phoenix, and J.A. Resko, "Influence of Gonadal Hormones on the Development and Activation of the Nervous System of the Rhesus Monkey," in *Influence of Hormones on the Nervous System,* D.H. Ford, ed. (S. Karger, New York, 1971), pp. 404—405, 408.

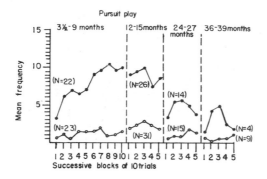

Figure 4. Frequency of pursuit play for normal male (● - ●) and female (o - o) rhesus monkeys during the first 3¼ years of life.

Source: E. Peretz, R.W. Goy, C.H. Phoenix, and J.A. Resko, "Influence of Gonadal Hormones on the Development and Activation of the Nervous System of the Rhesus Monkey," in *Influence of Hormones on the Nervous System*, D.H. Ford, ed. (S. Karger, New York, 1971), pp. 404—405, 408.

Dr. Goy interpreted such results to mean that early sexual dimorphisms, unlike those in the experimental rats, cannot be attributed to hormonal secretions present at birth but like the guinea pigs, must be due to some metabolic process that takes place prior to birth. To test this theory, Dr. Goy injected pregnant rhesus monkeys with the male hormone testosterone for twenty-five to fifty consecutive days. He found that genetic female offspring of such experiments showed uniformly malformed external genital structures, including well-developed scrotum, small but apparently complete penis, and obliteration of the external vaginal orifice. Further, the behavior of such pseudohermaphroditic females was markedly altered in the direction of normal male behavior. (See Figs. 5 and 6.) Frequency of "rough and tumble play" and "chasing play" were intermediate and overlapped with normal males; such "altered" females engaged in mounting behavior more than the normal females but less than the normal males. Dr. Goy interpreted the changes in behavior brought by the administration of male hormones to fetal female monkeys to mean that the male hormones act in some way on the developing nervous system.

The action is such that the individual infant, whether a genetic male or female, then is predisposed to behave in a manner that normally characterizes the genetic male.

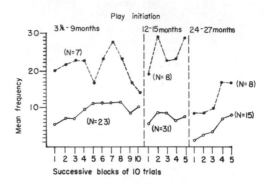

Figure 5. Frequency of play initiation for pseudohermaphroditic (● - ●) and normal (o - o) female rhesus monkeys during the first 2¼ years of life.

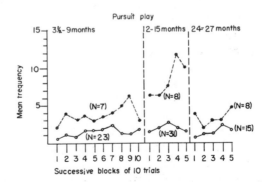

Figure 6. Frequency of pursuit play for pseudohermaphroditic (● - ●) and normal (o - o) female rhesus monkeys during the first 2¼ years of life.

Source: E. Peretz, R.W. Goy, C.H. Phoenix, and J.A. Resko, "Influence of Gonadal Hormones on the Development and Activation of the Nervous System of the Rhesus Monkey," in *Influence of Hormones on the Nervous System,* D.H. Ford, ed. (S. Karger, New York, 1971), pp. 404—405, 408.

The Hypothalamus

The next question was what mechanisms or processes are involved in the sexual dimorphism of the infant monkey's nervous system? Recent investigations by several investigators (Harris, 1964; Goy, 1968; Morey, 1968; Jensen, 1969) have suggested that the action of male hormones is centered in a part of the brain that is evolutionally quite old—the hypothalamus. Located in front of the brain stem, above the roof of the mouth in man, the hypothalamus is involved in the regulation of such vital functions as body temperature, blood pressure, sugar and coagulant levels in the blood, hunger, and thirst. It is also involved in the regulation of heart beat and other aspects of the well-known "flight or fight" response, including terror, anxiety, and even serenity. As the master control of the pituitary gland, which has been incorrectly called the "master gland" of the body, the hypothalamus is critical in the regulation of such important endocrine functions as body growth and sexual activity. As a result of the experiments by Dr. Goy and others, researchers now believe that all mammals studied thus far, including man, begin life with what is essentially a "female" hypothalamus with the capacity to initiate cyclically the release by the pituitary of hormones that induce ovulation. All hypothalamuses will function in this manner unless a male hormone, testosterone, is present in sufficient concentration at critical periods in the development of the brain to induce in effect the male pattern in the hypothalamus. The male pattern is, of course, noncyclical and does not have the capacity to induce ovulation. Once the male pattern has been induced, it cannot be reversed to the female pattern. Conversely, once the critical development period has passed for the induction of the male pattern, the hypothalamus will forever remain female in its orientation, although ovulation itself can be blocked by later administration of male hormones.

Several reports recently emphasize the degree of difference between "male" and "female" hypothalamuses. While the middle portion of the male and female hypothalamuses appear quite similar, the posterior and anterior portions, as well as nearby structures (such as the preoptic area), differ significantly in neural connections (Dorner & Staudt, 1968), protein content (Scacchi et al., 1970), and oxygen metabolism (Moguilevsky et al., 1968).

Beyond this, there is newly emerging evidence that the action of sex hormones, particularly testosterone, is not confined to the hypothalamus alone. A recent report from Brazil by Ladonsky and Gaziri (1970) suggests that the presence or absence of male hormones in infant rats is related to the level of serotonin in the brain, a vital substance believed to be involved in the transmission of information from one nerve cell to another. These investigators found that concentrations of serotonin in the brains of newborn rats remain constant to the eighth day of life, began to rise significantly in females on the twelfth day, but remained constant in normal males. In males castrated at birth, however, levels rose on the twelfth day as in females. This parallels a report that at sixty days of age, concentrations of 5-hydroxytryptamin, a monoamine and another nerve conductor, were higher in females than in males and that such differences are related to the action of sex hormones (Hyyppa, 1971).

Additional studies have also revealed that lesioning of certain portions of the brains of four-day-old rats differentially affects males and females, causing a delay in the onset of puberty in females but not in males (Relkin, 1971).

In rats, female sex hormones have been found to act directly on certain areas of the brain during the night of behavioral estrus and produce a decrease in rapid eye movement sleep; such changes in sleep do not occur when female hormones are administered to males (Branchey et al., 1971).

Sex differences in accumulation of amino acid in rats' brains have also been found and these differences are believed to be dependent on the actions of male hormones (Kartzinel et al., 1971). Sex differences in RNA concentration in specific areas of the rat brain have also been observed (Soriero and Ford, 1971). This research dealing with masculinization of the brain in a variety of laboratory animals suggests that there are indeed significant differences between males and females in their predisposition to engage in a variety of behaviors. It further suggests that modern research is providing a good deal of insight into the biological basis of these behavioral differences. In addition, it must be assumed that these differences, like all biological differences, are ultimately attributable to the operation of evolutionary forces. Young male monkeys are more aggressive and engage in more "rough and tumble play" than females because ground dwelling male monkeys must fight their way to their natural position in the dominance hierarchy of the group. The existence of such a hierarchy insures that the most vigorous and aggressive members of the group will not only do most of the reproducing, but will defend the group against predators and enemies and will be available to settle internal group squabbles. Such behavior further insures not only a union of the sexes but also females, as well as males, who will be physically and behaviorally capable of conceiving and rearing young. To the extent that these biological mechanisms help the animals succeed in these functions, are such traits favored by impersonal forces of evolution.

Sex Differences in General Human Behavior

It is of course quite difficult to determine if similar sexual differences exist in human male and female young. All human societies make distinctions between young male and females and such distinctions are certain to exhibit some effect on the learned behavior of children. The Israeli kibbutzim, however, make a deliberate effort to play down sex differences in the raising of children. The children are reared in peer groups primarily by female nurses and to some extent different sex socializers so common in other societies are absent. Yet, in studying the interaction patterns of children in kibbutzim, Spiro (1958) found many interesting differences in the interaction patterns of boys and girls (which parallel those found in monkeys).

> In all (age) groups girls are more integrative (give aid, share, act affectionate, cooperate, etc.) than boys, and boys more disintegrative. In all groups boys engage in more acts of conflict (seizure of another child's possessions) than girls, and in all but one group the boys engage in more acts of aggression (disobedience, hitting, insulting, etc.) than girls. Boys, moreover, are the recipients of the girls' excess integrations—boys are integrated more than girls—but girls are recipients of only part of the boys' excess disintegration. For though girls are the more frequent victims of conflict, boys are the more frequent victims of aggression.

Spiro's general conclusion is that many of these sex differences observed in the behavior of children are best accounted for by the innate sex-linked behavior hypothesis.

Comparisons between the behavior of rats and monkeys and that of humans may be challenged on the basis that the gulf between humans and the lower animals is so vast that it cannot be bridged by such logic. As noted previously, there is truth in this argument, but it must be tended with care. It is true that there are significant differences between men and animals, especially rats. But by the same token, it is also true that we have a good deal in common with the lower animals, especially the primates. And it is also true that human beings have too long indulged in the luxury of believing they are not animals. As B.F. Skinner has recently said, we are closer to pigs than angels, and I would add that we are in reality a whole lot closer to the monkeys in Dr. Goy's experiments than we are to any present commonly held conception of ourselves. As I heard one prominent physical anthroplogist remark recently, "Man in his behavior is probably as programmed as a duck; it is just that the programming is a whole lot more complicated."

Sex Differences in Human Sexual Behavior

In at least some segments of Western culture a well-known stereotype describes differences in the sexual nature of men and women. The male in this stereotype is strong and silent, not easily given to expressions of affection; and frequently is more concerned with the sex act itself than affectionate play either before or after sex. The female, on the other hand, is thought to be gentle and loving and less concerned with the orgastic pleasures of the sex act and more concerned with expressions of intimacy and warmth which usually accompany coitus. In this view, men and women are somewhat at odds with each other; the male desires to hurry along with the sex act and once finished sleeps or turns to other tasks; the female desires to prolong the more tender, as opposed to erotic, aspects of the relationship both prior to and following intercourse.

Many examples of this conflict can be found in literature. One example appears in Ernest Hemingway's short story, "Up in Michigan" (1938). Jim Gilmore has just, against her somewhat mild protestations, seduced Liz Coats on the wooden floor of a warehouse. Jim's endurance is limited, and when he is finished he falls asleep still atop Liz. Hemingway concludes the story with a short description of Liz's behavior indicating on one hand her slight degree of contentment, yet on the other a sort of frustration, a longing for something more, something that Jim cannot provide.

> The hemlock planks of the dock were hard and splintery
> and cold and Jim was heavy on her and he had hurt her.
> Liz pushed him, she was so uncomfortable and

71

cramped. Jim was asleep. He wouldn't move. She worked out from under him and sat up and straightened her skirt and coat and tried to do something with her hair. Jim was sleeping with his mouth a little open. Liz leaned over and kissed him on the cheek. He was still asleep. She lifted his head a little and shook it. He rolled his head over and swallowed. Liz started to cry. She walked over to the edge of the dock and looked down to the water. There was a mist coming up from the bay. She was cold and miserable and everything felt gone. She walked back to where Jim was lying and shook him once more to make sure. She was crying.

"Jim," she said, "Jim, please, Jim."

Jim stirred and curled a little tighter. Liz took off her coat and leaned over and covered him with it. She tucked it around him neatly and carefully. Then she walked across the dock and up the steep sandy road to go to bed. A cold mist was coming up through the woods from the bay.

Jim's behavior would certainly not be in vogue in liberal quarters today, and if Liz were a modern sexually demanding female of the 1970s, Jim probably would not get the opportunity to enjoy her favors a second time. Nevertheless, there is a considerable body of evidence that suggests that Jim is not altogether the callous clod he appears and that Liz's response is probably a very normal female response. This new evidence suggests that there are indeed biological factors that seem to account for the differences in their behavior and that the old stereotype concerning sex response differences between men and women appears to have a physiological basis.

Effect of Hormones on Eroticism and Affection

The sex life of every adult is, to a great extent, determined by a sort of orchestration by the body of a number of sex hormones. The sex life of the male is largely determined by the action of male hormones on selected tissues. These male hormones (androgens) are produced by both the testes and the adrenal cortex. In contrast, the sex life of the female is believed to be determined by an interplay between female (estrogens) and male hormones. In the female most of the male hormones are produced by the adrenal cortex while most of the female hormones are produced by the ovaries.

Recent investigations on women who had either their ovaries or adrenals or both removed for the treatment of cancer suggest that the functions of female and male hormones in adult women are quite different (Drellich and Waxenberg, 1966). When only the adrenal glands are removed and women are consequently deprived of naturally produced male hormones, women consistently report a dramatic reduction in sex drive. There is almost a complete loss of erotic capacity. These women report feeling unsexed, with no sexual emotion or genital excitability. Women who have undergone this operation have stated, "I don't care if I ever have sex in my life again;" and "I couldn't care less about sex." These same women, however, report having a need for "nestling" and "closeness," and feel "compassion for men." The loss of the erotic response seemingly is accompanied by a continuation of the affectionate component of female sexuality.

When only the ovaries are removed and the primary source of estrogen is gone, however, the effect is the opposite. Women report little loss of sex drive and erotic capacity with completely normal sex lives.

Researchers have offered several theories for the effect that male hormones have on female eroticism. It has been suggested, for example, that male hormones increase vascularity of the vulva region and the sensitivity of the clitoris. A second theory suggests that male hormones might stimulate metabolism and increase sexual feelings secondary to increasing the sense of general well-being. Still a third theory suggests that male hormones might increase psychic sensitization and susceptibility to sexual stimuli (Drellich and Waxenberg, 1966).

If it is true that male hormones stimulate erotic needs and fire the sex drive, and female hormones stimulate affectional needs, then it is perfectly understandable that men are primarily concerned with the erotic component of sex while women are concerned with the interpersonal, affectionate component. Since males possess more male hormones than females, who would expect otherwise? And since females possess more female hormones than males one would also expect women to exhibit more of the behavioral traits that the female hormones seem to encourage. Further, there is great variability in individual hormone levels and patterns which are determined by genetics as well as environment. Thus, we should expect to find great variability in erotic and affectionate behavior among men and women. Undoubtedly the curve for variability in male eroticism overlaps with the curve for female eroticism and conversely for affectionate behavior. The fact is, however, that while the behavior curves for these two traits may overlap for the sexes, erotic behavior is more characteristic of males than females, and affectionate behavior is more characteristic of females than males.

The foregoing theory regarding the hormonal basis of human sexuality finds interesting confirmation in a report in *Scientific American* (August 1972, p. 46). Researchers at the University of Birmingham in England found that female rhesus monkeys in whom ovaries had been removed suffered no reduction in sex drive, although sex drive was markedly reduced in males with whom they were paired. When female adrenals were removed, however, there was a great reduction in sexual receptivity. The authors concluded that whereas among nonprimates the secretion of female sex hormones usually enhances sexual receptivity, among primates this function has been taken over by male hormones secreted by the adrenals. In primates, the authors suggest, female sex hormones serve the function of increasing the sexual attractiveness of the female.

An example of male versus female eroticism can be found in certain species of primates. While the introduction of a new male member into a group brings scarcely a glimmer of interest from the females, the introduction of a new female (in estrus) into the group arouses the males and leads to temporary neglect of the other females.

In view of this, the liberated women's advertisement of their erotic capacities (an act reserved for the male of the species) seems to indicate one of three things: (1) abnormal environment has seriously distorted these women's natural sexual tendencies and capacities; (2) excessive male hormones produced by overactive adrenal and/or underactive ovaries (certainly the size and features of many of these women suggest this); or (3) a combination of (1) or (2). In any case eroticism seems to be the natural forte of males, and one can only view with concern those women who have lost account of this fact.

The theory regarding the different roles that ovarian and adrenal cortical hormones play in the female sexual response also has implications for understanding a commonly observed trait in postmenopausal women. It is a widespread belief in popular culture that women past the menopause often become unaffectionate, cold, nonempathetic, and in general lack warmth toward others, especially males. While this belief is probably partly attributable to a stereotype, it seems that like most stereotypes it is partially factual. Certainly my own experience and those of many persons with whom I have talked convinces me that there is some truth in the belief. One never hears of a "young hag;" it is always an "old hag." The expressions "old bag" and "old bitch" are well known. Might it be that much of the "warmth" and "affectional" component of female character is in part due to the influence of ovarian hormones, and that once these hormones are lost at the female "change of life," there is a reduction in that aspect of female character? She ceases to be cuddly, empathetic, and motherly and becomes hard, brittle, and more sour, like good wine turned to vinegar. It may be that such an individual was always a lemon—in her youth she was the same. Such an observation fits the theory. A sour woman in youth can be expected to become more sour in middle and old age, for even as a youth she suffers from relative "deficiency" of the vital ovarian hormones; after menopause she is worse compared to her counterpart who had an abundance of these hormones in youth.

The Brain and Sexual Stimuli

Recent experiments (MacLean, 1965, 1966) conducted on squirrel monkeys indicate the possibility of an anatomical basis for the fact that men and women are sexually aroused by a variety of stimuli not directly related to the sexual act. These experiments help account for the fact that human sexual behavior frequently involves oral activities such as kissing and oral sex, anal manipulation and analinguis, and olfactory stimulation such as the use of perfumes and natural body odors. It also might help explain why some individuals are sexually aroused by inflicting pain upon themselves or others and why there is sometimes an association between sex and aggressive attack. These seemingly diverse behaviors appear to have a physiological basis. In experiments on squirrel monkeys, Dr. P.D. MacLean has noted that the limbic lobe, a bundle of nerves located deep within the brain is bent around itself. The bending of the limbic lobe has the effect of bringing into close anatomical proximity areas of brain tissue that relate to oral, olfactory, anal, and genital functions. Close associations also exist between brain tissue responsible for regulation of aggressive and sexual functions. Dr. MacLean found, for example, that stimulation of the region involved in oral function readily spilled over into the area concerned with genital function.

Effect of Hormones on Stress

There are striking dissimilarities in the number of sex hormones that the organs manufacture. In the mature adult female of child-bearing age, the ovaries produce approximately 85 percent of the female estrogen hormones; the remaining 15 percent are produced by the cortex of the adrenal gland. In adult males the pattern of production is quite different. The testes produce only 35 percent of the male androgen hormones, while the adrenal cortex produces 65 percent (Tintera, 1968). In addition to sex hormones, however, the cortex of the adrenal, the outer layer of the small almond-shaped organ which is astride both of the kidneys, also produces a large number of two other kinds of hormones. (Including sex hormones the adrenal cortex is known to produce at least 41 different hormones, most, of course, in extremely minute amounts.) The other two types of hormones, in addition to sex hormones, that are produced by the adrenal cortex are those that are responsible for the regulation of carbohydrate metabolism and those that help regulate mineral metabolism. Since the primary function of the adrenal cortical hormones is to keep the metabolic forces of the body in balance, they are, in both men and women, the first line of defense against any form of stress or shock. The adrenal glands of most individuals though, have a limited capacity to produce the hormones necessary to cope with stress. Therefore, prolonged stress (i.e., heat, cold, tension, etc.) can lead to dangerous weakening or even complete exhaustion of the adrenal cortex' capacity. This weakening may cause diseases including arthritis, liver and heart abnormalities, hypoglycemia, some forms of mental illness, alcoholism, and general lack of vigor and vitality. Complete exhaustion of the adrenals' capacity to produce hormones is known as Addison's disease and quickly results in death if these hormones are not supplemented medically.

Since there are striking differences between men and women in the proportion of the total load of sex hormones that the adrenals are forced to carry, it can be argued that there are important differences between the sexes in their capacity to handle stress. Since the adrenal glands of adult females of child-bearing age do not carry as heavy a burden of sex hormones as adult males, women probably have more resistance than men to many varieties of stress at that period of their lives. At a given level of stress, the female adrenal cortex is working under a lighter burden. Again this makes great evolutionary sense; women can handle stress better while they are capable of replenishing the species.

This fact, John W. Tintera (1969), the late endocrinologist, contended is the reason that there are fewer female alcoholics than male alcoholics prior to the age of female menopause. However, following menopause, at which time the ovaries stop producing estrogen, the entire burden of female hormones productions falls on the adrenal cortex. Consequently, after menopause, women are less able to cope with stress than men. (The adrenals in males are still carrying their relatively smaller burdens.) Dr. Tintera felt this accounts for the dramatic increase in rates of alcoholism in post-menopausal women.

It has also been demonstrated that chronic socially induced stress can affect the production of sex hormones. Investigators (*Science News*, May 20, 1972) at Walter Reed Army Hospital in Washington, D.C., compared the testosterone levels of eighteen officer candidates enrolled in a twenty-three-week officer candidate training program with a control group not under such stress. During the first twelve weeks of the program, the candidates were under intense stress. During the last four weeks stress was greatly reduced and the candidates enjoyed new status and privileges. Measurements of plasma testosterone revealed that during the third week of the program testosterone levels of the candidates fell an average of 32 percent in comparison to the non-stressed control group. During the twenty-second week, however, candidates' male hormones levels were comparable to those of the control group. Perhaps these findings help explain why wives of executives frequently complain of reduced libido in their husbands. In addition, possibilities of high stress levels and reduced male hormones production being related to the often commented on femininization of the American male are intriguing.

Role of Environment in Sexual Response

We have seen that in the animal kingdom it is nature's first intent to produce a female. This makes good evolutionary sense. In terms of the survival of a species of animals the presence of a large number of females in a group is much more important than the presence of a large number of males. Among most mammals one male can service more than one female during a season, but a female can negotiate only one pregnancy at a time. When a rancher desires to increase the size of his herd of cattle or sheep, the birth of males disappoints him; the birth of females delights him.

Nature's favoritism for the female can be seen in the results of a large number of experiments that attempted to disrupt the sexual response in mammals. Experiments on mice, rats, cats, dogs, and various species of primates demonstrate that it is more difficult to disrupt the female sexual response than the male response. Among rodents and carnivores, females continue to copulate despite the destruction of massive areas of cortex in the brain. However, the destruction of even moderate amounts of brain matter in males leads to a complete cessation of the male sexual response; in such cases, males are completely incapable of being aroused sexually. Experiments on a number of sub-primate species of animals (Beach, 1947) demonstrates that females are capable of fertile copulation after combined removal of organs for vision, olfaction, and hearing, and respond sexually to the appropriate stimulation provided by direct bodily contact with a sexually active male. Sexual stimulation of males of these same species, however, is dependent not on a single sensory cue as in the female, but on a pattern of stimulation involving simultaneous and repetitive action of several sensory systems. Regarding the effect of environment on sexual behavior in these species, Beach (1947) found that strange and familiar environments that have previously been associated with painful stimulation inhibits male sexual behavior much more than female sexual behavior. Environments in which successful copulation has taken place facilitate the sexual response of the male but not the female. Once the male becomes aroused, he is not responsive to extraneous, nonsexual environmental stimuli, however, whereas the female is. In an outstanding review article dealing with the physiology of maleness and femaleness, Dr. Warren J. Gadpaille (1972) pointed out that much the same results have been achieved in experiments on primates. Among chimpanzees, sexually inexperienced females are more capable of copulation; males have to learn. Destruction of the male chimpanzee's cerebral cortex (brain tissue) destroyed the male's capacity to copulate. The same damage did not affect the female's capacity. The male primate's dependence on learning, as opposed to the female's independence, is further underlined by several experiments on the effects of primate social life and adult sexual behavior. Dr. Harry Harlow's famous work (1962, 1965) on rhesus monkeys reveals that individual mothering, formal peer group social contact, and sex play during childhood are all important to the development of normal sexual behavior in adults. Unsatisfactory mothering experiences were less important because their negative effects could be overcome by peer experiences. Lack of peer experiences, however, results in irreparable sexual incapacities. None of the males ever developed normal adult sexual behavior; a few females, however, did, and their partial recovery was made possible by the actions of normal experienced, adult males who were quite patient with the females. Research efforts directed at raising chimpanzees in isolation reveals much the same results. Following periods of social deprivation between puberty and adulthood, females learned to copulate with the assistance of experienced males. Male inabilities cannot be overcome, however.

Numerous researchers have interpreted these findings to mean that male sexual behavior is intimately influenced by the cerebral cortex, the higher learning centers of the brain, whereas female sexual behavior is controlled by the more primitive and evolutionally older parts of the brain. In females, sexual behavior is more   reflexive and less dependent on learning and environment. Among males sexual ability is more refined, more delicate, more subject to the influences of environment.

Development of Masculinity

These important studies form the core of a newly emerging view of human sexuality. They tell us that there are very basic differences between males and females in terms of the origins of their sexuality. The fact that all animals begin life as females and that males are produced only when male hormones are present to transform the female-like fetal tissues to the male form indicates that the development of masculinity is more complex than the development of femininity. Biologically the male form represents additional steps taken by nature to modify the basic female form. Any time nature must take additional steps to develop a life form, the probability that something can go wrong increases. Thus from a biological point of view, nature can make more mistakes in developing males than females. Since the development of masculine sexual behavior is more dependent on learning, the male is additionally disadvantaged. As the studies on lower animals demonstrate, normal female sexual identity and behavior emerge despite the fact that the top half of the female's head is in effect removed. Nature has built into the creation of female sexuality a large margin for error;

many mistakes can be made in the development of female sexuality, yet there is assurance that the end product will be a reasonable facsimile of a normally functioning female. There is no such assurance for the development of male sexuality. The male must not only have his higher mental functions intact to perform normally, but he also must undergo the proper environmental experiences at the proper time. If both factors are not present, a deficiency of masculinity and masculine behavior are the result. From any perspective, the development of the normal male is much more subject to the winds of chance and vicissitudes of environment than the development of a comparable state in females. Put in simple terms, all the evidence points to the fact that it is much more difficult to become a normal male than a normal female. This fact probably accounts for the higher rate of sexual perversions among males. Dr. Warren J. Gadpaille (1972), for example, has noted that few experts would deny that homosexuality is more prevalent in men than in women, and the disparity is even higher when it comes to such increasingly bizarre perversions as fetishism, sadism, masochism, and animal contacts as well as other deviations such as necrophilia which are found only in males. The difficulty of being a male is compounded by the fact that the male must frequently initiate a sexual liaison and be physically prepared for coitus. This is much less true for the female. As Dr. Gadpaille notes, ". . .a female may passively submit to coitus with minimal participation and in the face of multifarious sexual fears and conflict, and yet conceive and fulfill her reproductive function, whereas a male can perform his procreative function only under complex and emotionally supportive conditions in which it is possible for him to attain erection, maintain it adequately for intromission, and ejaculate; the hazards to male sexual functioning are legion. (p. 202)" Male inadequacy is more visible.

·Initiation Rites

Societies that we usually regard as unsophisticated in these matters appear to have been very much aware of the special problems males face in achieving their rightful sexual identity. Many cultures around the world have developed special techniques designed to assist young men in achieving their identity. For some time there has been a rather heated debate among anthropologists as to the function of puberty initiation rights in primitive societies. A number of societies sponsor parallel initiation rites for both males and females; but rites for males are much more common and much more highly featured. A puberty ceremony in a primitive society usually involves the induction of the initiate into a secret society with the culture or generally signals the initiate's emergence into manhood. The ceremony usually involves the infliction of psychic or physical pain on the youth. Pain is inflicted in a variety of ways including isolation, hazards, endurance tests, and circumcision (one of the most common); laceration of the skin and removal of teeth are also practiced. The practice among some Australian aborigines of making an incision along the length of the underside of the penis completely through to the urethra, known as subincision, is certainly one of the more spectacular and painful.

Three theories have been offered by anthropologists to account for the existence of initiation rites. One theory offered by Dr. John Whiting and associates (1961) at Harvard University notes that circumcision around the world is associated with the practice of mother and child sleeping together apart from the father for a protracted period following the birth of the child, in this case a male. Dr. Whiting suggests that the circumcision of the male in the ceremony that marks the transition from boyhood to manhood is an effort to break the cross-sex identification that the boy has acquired as a result of sleeping with his mother and instill in him an identification with men. A second theory, proposed by Dr. Frank Young (1962), states that the function of the ceremony is to dramatize and reinforce the social solidarity of adult males. Dr. Young has pointed out that such ceremonies tend to take place in environments where food resources are limited and where those resources must be exploited through cooperative groups. In a third theory Dr. John Greenway (1963) has suggested that the initiation ceremony is in effect a dramatic means of getting the boy's attention. As a result of such attention-getting devices, the youth is less likely to forget the valuable information concerning the male role which is imparted him during the ceremony. This theory certainly makes sense in terms of the known relationship between elevated levels of stress and increased efficiency of learning.

While these three theories dealing with the function of male initiation differ slightly in their emphasis, they are all concerned essentially with the impartation of adult male values and behavior on the young males. The practices indicate, in effect, that the developing male frequently needs an assist from society in order to attain his masculine identity. These cultures have learned that if the male is not assisted at such times the identity does not fully develop and the society suffers. These primitive cultures know that while the male has an inborn quest for masculinity, the success of the quest is dependent on environmental factors. To fail to assist the male in the quest for his identity is tantamount to the cultivation of a misfit, a creature neither male or female, a burden to society and survival. Female initiation ceremonies can be explained in the same way. They assist the female in achieving her female identity. But, since the emergence of female identity involves fewer factors, is less dependent on environment, is more dependent on the unfolding of innate biological factors, the female needs less assistance from society. Thus female initiation ceremonies are less common than male and do not have nearly the social importance.

The Male in American Society

It is obvious from this discussion that American society has things backwards. In this society, we take masculine identity for granted. The male is expected to be constantly in pursuit of the female; his masculine ego-identity is thought to be made of stone; he is expected to be eternally virile; and he is expected to be ready to copulate at any time, any place, under any circumstances. If he cannot satisfy the most frigid, asexual woman, he is inadequate. The female, on the other hand, is seen as a poor, weak creature whose sexual identity is as fragile as a flower. Before she can have sex everything must be exactly right; each cup and saucer must be in its proper place. She must be complimented; she must be petted; she must be fondled; her ego must be flattered; and in many cases, money must be spent on her. If she is frigid, the male must remain eternally patient; if she is a nymphomaniac, he must have the stamina of a marathon runner. In America, masculinity is seen as constant and unvarying; femininity is seen as highly variable and dependent on the environment.

In our society the male is given no quarter in his efforts to achieve his masculine identity. Nearly all attempts to achieve masculinity are met with ridicule and disparagement. If a male attempts to set himself apart from women, he is called a showoff, a chauvinist, or an inadequate. If he cultivates masculine interests, he is said to be compensating psychologically for some deeply buried inferiority, perhaps constitutional. If he attempts to achieve his identity through the seduction of women, he is said to be a latent homosexual. If he attempts to exert his natural tendency to dominate (especially women), he is authoritarian, low-class, and uneducated.

There are virtually no ceremonies to proclaim to society the validity of the male's masculinity, few ceremonies to cultivate it or to stabilize it. The young male's natural tendency to engage in more rough and tumble play is called unruly and rowdy; he may even be diagnosed as hyperactive and given drugs to "settle him down." The only avenue open to the male for expression of his masculinity is competitive sports. If he is unable to participate in competition, he does so vicariously in the grandstands or before the TV. But he even pays a price here: his penchant for long hours of TV football is subject to much ridicule.

The women's liberationist movement is merely an acceleration of the successful attempt to cut from modern society even the most inconspicuous masculine traits.

Recent Cases of Impotence

Psychiatrists have recently noted an increase in the number of young unmarried males complaining of intense anxiety and sexual impotence (Ginsberg, 1972). Suffering from weak masculine identities to begin with, these young men have developed impotence early in their relationships with "newly freed" women who demand sexual performance. Commenting on this development recently in the *Archives of General Psychiatry*, a group of New York psychiatrists stated:

> When we explored these sexual failures occurring early in a relationship, we found a common male complaint: these newly freed women demanded sexual performance. The male concern of the 1940s and 1950s was to satisfy the woman. In the late 1960s and 1970s, it seems to be, "Will I have to maintain an erection to maintain a relationship?" This idea is permeated with feelings of "who calls the shots" and "who is sex for." There is a reversal of former roles: the role of the put-upon Victorian woman is that of a put-upon man on the 1970s. "Whereas a man's impotence is obvious, a woman's frigidity can be hidden." Inhibited nonorgastic women can often hide their lack of response but men without erect penises cannot even feign intromission. This challenge to manhood is most apparent in a sexually liberated society where women are not merely available but are perceived as demanding satisfaction from masculine performance. (Ginsberg, 1972, p. 219).

Reports of impotency among males with dominating female partners are not limited to New York City. Dr. J. M. Stewart, writing in the medical magazine *Pulse*, has noted that an increasing number of male students at Oxford University in England are becoming impotent and that such impotency can be attributed to "the reversal of sex roles, with women taking a more positive part." (*Denver Post*, July 24, 1972) The human male's response of impotency when confronted with a dominating female is of special interest in view of a recent study conducted by Drs. L. A. Rosenblum and R. D. Nadler (1971) of the Department of Psychiatry, Downstate Medical Center, State University of New York, Brooklyn, on the sexual behavior of male bonnet macaque monkeys. These researchers found that, "If the male is not sufficiently dominant over the female, sexual behavior will be inhibited or disrupted. (p. 398)" It was found, for example, that when a receptive female was placed in the cage of a mature male who was larger and more dominant than the female, the male almost immediately moved towards her, mounted her in the ventral-dorsal position, grasping her calves with his feet and her hips with his hands, and began vigorous rapid thrusting. Intromission occurred and ejaculation usually took place on the first, or at least immediately succeeding, mount. Following a period of quiescence, a second sexual interaction usually occurred.

Adolescent males performed as mature males when placed with smaller females over whom they were dominant. When placed with females larger than themselves, however, females over whom they were not dominant, they became timid and often failed to express any sexual behavior. Frequently, they fought with the females, often losing the encounter. In their study of the sexual behavior of male macaque monkeys, the authors conclude that ". . . the estimation of behavioral capacities at various ages may be influenced dramatically by the failure to consider the dominance question." It seems reasonable to suppose that the same may be said of man in his relations with woman.

Homosexuality

> For gay people, the essential point is to see limited sexuality as an end result of male supremacy and sex roles. Gay, in its most far-reaching sense, means not homosexual, but sexually free. This includes a long-range vision of sensuality as a basis for sexual relationships. . .It may be utopian to think that all people who now define themselves as "straight" will become gay, but it is not utopian to ask people who call themselves revolutionaries to struggle against sexism by working toward establishing a gay identity and combating male power . . . "Two, four, six, eight, gay is twice as good as straight! (Allen Young, "A Gay Manifesto," *Ramparts Magazine*, November, 1971)

> For lesbians, Women's Liberation is not an intellectual or emotional luxury, but a personal imperative. (Sidney Abbott and Barbara Soal, *Sappho Was A Right-on Woman: A Liberated View of Lesbianism*)

Many investigators who have written in the area of the masculinization of the hypothalamus in animals have noted the obvious implications that such findings have for the understanding and perhaps eventual treatment of homosexuality in man. Using the theory of adrenal exhaustion as a touchstone, a graduate student at UCLA, John F. Tholen (1970) developed a theory that might account not only for one of the many forms of male homosexuality but also its origins. This theory may also provide some insight into the "de-masculinization" of the American male.

It is known that male hormones are necessary for the masculinization of the genetic male fetus. If such hormones are not present at the critical period of development, the male infant will be born with what amounts to a female hypothalamus and what are probably its many metabolic and behavioral implications. It is also known that adrenocortical hormones are capable of crossing the placental barrier between mother and unborn child. In the case of hormone deficiencies, such as diabetes, it is known that a deficient mother will in effect "pirate" a portion of the insulin that the developing fetus manufactures. This explains, in part, why many diabetic women feel fine sometimes and do not need medication while pregnant, but experience a recurrence of symptoms following the birth of the infant. In view of this, Tholen has suggested that when a woman deficient in adrenocortical hormones is pregnant with a genetic male fetus the mother might begin "stealing" the infant's adrenocortical hormones for her own use. If the child has a weak adrenocortical system to begin with, and we know that there is a wide variability among people with regard to such traits, then at the crucial time of masculinization, there might not be sufficient male hormones to fully masculinize the young male's hypothalamus. The individual would be forever burdened with part of his nervous system functioning as a female. It also seems reasonable to suppose that in a percentage of such cases the hypothalamus might be partially masculinized but not fully so. Such a situation might result in an individual who is bisexual or a male who feels weak and uncomfortable in the traditional male dominant role. Such individuals might acquiesce to a variety of individual and socially dominating forces (including some of the vitriol of Women's Liberation) and might find himself participating with great fervor in Women's Liberation and perhaps even Gay Liberation.

This theory is compatible with the fact that environmentalists in psychology and psychiatry have failed rather dramatically in attempts to understand homosexuality from an environmental and learning point of view. One researcher, after failing to establish environmental causes of the disease, concluded that male homosexuality was due to "some factor within the homosexual himself." Tholen's theory is also compatible with the stereotype of the homosexual who has more delicate features, stature, body movements, and an above- average I.Q. The latter trait is especially interesting in view of Dr. Tintera's (1969) suspicion that persons suffering from adrenocortical hormonal insufficiency seem to show frequency of above-average intelligence.

The view that homosexuality is a result of an abnormal environment between mother and unborn offspring finds corroboration in a recent report in *Science* (Ward, 1972). In experiments with rats, Dr. Ingeborg L. Ward found that adult male rats whose mothers had been exposed to high levels of stress while pregnant with the males exhibited lower levels of male sexual behavior. She also found these same males exhibited a significant increase in clearly defined female sexual behavior. Levels of stress following birth of the males was found to be unrelated to such abnormal behavior. Dr. Ward explains her results by noting that the male hormones produced by the adrenals are weaker and less potent than those produced by the testes. She believes that under stress the abundance of hormones produced by both the mother and the fetus, cause an alteration in the normal ratio of male hormones in the unborn and thus prevent full masculinization of the brain.

The suggestion that homosexuality actually involves biological abnormalities takes on added importance in view of an editorial and some findings recently published in *The New England Journal of Medicine* (Federman, 1971; Kolodny, 1971). Male hormone (plasma testosterone) levels of thirty healthy homosexual male college students were assayed and compared to the hormone levels of fifty healthy male heterosexual college students. Homosexual students were categorized according to a scale developed by the late Dr. A. C. Kinsey, with those predominantly heterosexual but occasionally homosexual at one end of the scale and those predominately or exclusively homosexual at the other end of the scale. The researchers found no difference in the hormone levels between the heterosexual college students and those homosexuals who engaged in heterosexual relationships at least as frequently as homosexual. Hormone levels of the homosexuals who were predominantly or exclusively homosexual however were quite low—halfway between the normal heterosexual students and samples of normal women. In addition, sperm counts in the homosexuals varied according to degree of homosexuality; sperm counts in those predominantly or exclusively homosexual were impaired or absent. Authors also note other research where elevated urinary testosterone levels have been found in female homosexuals.

These findings clearly show that the penchant in Latin cultures to judge an adult male's masculinity in terms of the number of children he has sired has an element of scientific validity. Low male hormone levels appear to correlate with homosexuality and low sperm counts.

If these findings and interpretations stand the test of further investigation, homosexuality should not be viewed as a state of liberation for either of the sexes. It should instead be seen as a condition of physical malfunction, which leads to behavior that, from a biological and evolutionary point of view, is maladaptive. From this point of view, a homosexual is not to be either admired or despised for his behavior; he should be pitied along with the individual born with birth defects or the victim of multiple sclerosis. Talk of converting the majority of society to homosexuality is nonsense and will only occur in the most pathological kind of environments. As Dr. Warren J. Gadpaille (1972) has noted,

> Preferential homosexuality is clearly a result of some disorder in the normally programmed sequence of psychosexual differentiation and development, however early or subtle the interference may be. The growing comprehension of the normal sequence leading to biologically appropriate sexually dimorphic identification and behavior makes an ever more lucid case for the necessity for one or another kind of interference to cause an abiological maladaptation such as homosexuality. (p. 203)

For these reasons, homosexuals should not be allowed to exhibit and flaunt their unnatural behaviors in public. What they do in the privacy of their homes is their business, but they should not be permitted to serve as positive role models for children, especially boys, who are in the process of attempting to evolve their own normal sexual identity.

The Premenstrual Syndrome

It is common belief that adult women, and to a lesser extent adult men, are sometimes subject to violent periodic fluctuations in mood and body functions. These fluctuations in women have long been associated with the menstrual cycle. Because many of the arguments and social programs of the Women's Liberationists hinge on the contention that there are no significant differences, other than obvious anatomical ones, between men and women, it is of some interest to attempt to determine whether the mood and body changes so frequently thought to accompany the menstrual cycle are the result of cultural conditioning or innate culture-free biological processes.

There can be little doubt that human females do experience periodic mental and body changes that are correlated with their menstrual cycles. The roster of female complaints and ailments that physicians and psychiatrists see are legion. In general most of the complaints cluster in the period just prior to the onset of menstruation. Frequently, there is a gradual onset of symptoms a few days prior to menstruation, and they may persist for the first one to three days when the menstrual flow is light. Usually there is an abrupt cessation of symptoms with the onset of full menstruation. In England, Katharina Dalton (1964) refers to this widespread problem as "the premenstrual syndrome," as opposed to the more common term of "premenstrual tension," tension being but one aspect of the syndrome. In addition to tension, Dalton describes other psychological characteristics of the syndrome: irritability, depression, lethargy, alcoholic excess, nymphomania, distortion phenomena, feelings of unreality, and sleep disturbances. Physical symptoms include headache, epilepsy, vertigo, syncope, asthma, engorgement of the nasal mucous membrane, hoarseness, nausea and vomiting, constipation, hemorrhoids, colicky pain, Mittelschmerz (mild cramping pain in the iliac fossa caused by rupture of the Graafian follicle at ovulation), abdominal bloatedness, increased appetite, hypoglycemia, oliguria, enuresis, urinary retention, joint and muscle pains, metatarsalgia (pain in metarsal bones of foot), heart palpitations, varicose veins, capillary fragility, dermatological lesions, breast enlargement, pain and tenderness, reddening and watering of the eyes, styes, and glaucoma. In addition, resistance to viral and bacterial infections is also impaired (Luce, 1971, p. 110). Given the numerous mental and physical changes, it would be unthinkable to suppose that the premenstrual syndrome would not also include some observable behavior changes. Actually there is considerable scientific literature documenting this fact. Katharina Dalton, in a review of some of this literature, states the following:

> The common symptoms of premenstrual tension, lethargy, irritability and depression, becomes reflected in the day-to-day behavior of many women and girls. The presence of symptoms on some days and their absence on other days of the month all serve to account for the unpredictable enigma of woman, as she appears to her menfolk. Several surveys on the effect of menstruation upon behavior suggest that the influence of the premenstrual syndrome is widespread in our English population and that its far reaching effects are not yet properly understood or appreciated. (p. 77)

Dalton herself has conducted a number of studies of the relationship between school girls' monthly cycles and their behavior. In one English boarding school where it was customary to keep records of dates of bad behavior and dates of menstruation, analysis showed a statistically significant increase of frequencies of bad behavior during the four days of menstruation. It was also found that when designated girls were allowed to punish others girls for misbehavior, standards of discipline tended to raise during menstruation of the then disciplinarians and then gradually fall during the remainder of the cycle. Other observations of English school girls, aged ten to fourteen, revealed a drop in tidiness of bed and drawer during menstruation where the observers were unaware of the observed girls' cycles.

Dalton has also conducted research on adult female behavior. One study of 156 newly-convicted prisoners revealed that 49 percent were sentenced for crimes committed during premenses. Twenty-seven percent of the 157 (Dalton's figures 156 vs 157) prisoners suffered from the premenstrual syndrome and 63 percent of this group committed their crimes during premenses. Further, among prisoners reported for misbehavior while in prison, 70 percent of the offenses occurred during premenses. Concerning the relationship between menstruation and deviance in prisoners and school girls, Dalton says the data show ". . .the close similarity of the effect of menstruation on naughty school girls, newly-convicted prisoners and disorderly prisoners. The offenses for which the naughty school girls were published are altogether different from those crimes for which a prison sentence is passed. The hormonal changes associated with menstruation render the individual less amenable to discipline, more tense and less alert, so that she is more likely to be detected in her misdoings." (p. 80)

Other researchers have found a relationship between the menstrual cycle and moods (Moos et al., 1969), between food cravings and depression (Smith and Sauder, 1969), and dream content (Swanson and Foulkes, 1968). Anxiety, depression, aggression, pleasantness, and activation were found to change cyclically in relation to the menstrual cycle; cravings for sweets and other foods were thought to be associated with premenstrual tensions and depression; and dreams with manifest sexuality tended to be highest during menses. The cravings for sweets and other prementstrual symptoms of alcoholic excess and hypoglycemia are of more than passing interest in view of stress theory and hypoadrenocorticism discussed previously.

Actually all of this is really nothing new. In many quarters these facts have been well understood for a long time. Dalton cites a reference, for example, which suggests that the term "lunacy" reflects ancient knowledge of the association of abnormal female behavior with the phases of the moon (p. 77). In England, at Westfield State Prison, some women inmates are given the precautionary privilege of requesting to be locked in their rooms each month during the days of premenstrual tension, when mental instability is most dangerous and acute (Dalton, 1964, p. 82). In France premenstrual symptoms are recognized for legal purposes as temporary insanity.

This now brings us to the question of the origin of the "premenstrual syndrome" and whether it is found in all races and women of all cultures or limited in its distribution and restricted only to certain cultures in which these mental and physiological responses are "taught." One prominent anthropologist recently stuck his neck out and suggested that it was a "learned" response. In his introductory text to anthropology, Dr. Marvin Harris (1971) appears to place himself clearly in the camp of the environmentalists with the following statement:

> . . . the association between menstruation and irritability, depression and physical pain is not necessarily a biological given. What is given is a wide variation in psychological states associated with menstruation among women in different cultures (p. 583-4).

One way to determine the validity of the environmentalists position is to look at the biological underpinnings of the premenstrual syndrome. While little is known about the biochemistry, there is the suggestion that, as might be expected, the origins lie not with the reproductive organs but with the hypothalamus, that not only do the ovarian hormones fluctuate regularly throughout the normal menstrual cycle but that the adrenal cortex also exhibits cyclical activity. Adrenocortical hormones are known to increase in the week preceding menstruation. Dalton reviews the literature in which a number of researchers suggest that one of the primary factors in the etiology of the premenstrual syndrome is an imbalance between ovarian and adrenocortical hormones in the week preceding menstruation. Production of the adrenocortical hormone aldosterone is excessive in relation to ovarian hormones, causing the kidneys to retain too much sodium and excrete too much potassium. (Progesterone has an antagonistic effect on aldosterone.) The resultant mineral imbalance gives rise to the retention of water, which produces the swelling and edema, and presumably leads to many of the other symptoms. While such an explanation is far from complete, it clearly does point the way to a physiological as opposed to a cultural explanation for many of the problems associated with menstruation.

There is other evidence for a physiological explanation. Gay Gaer Luce (1971), in an outstanding volume dealing with biological rhythms in man and animals, cites research conducted by Dr. Oscar Janiger of the University of California at Irvine. In one research project Dr. Janiger administered a questionnaire to zoo keepers which led to the realization that rhesus monkeys, chimpanzees, and gorillas appear to exhibit the same premenstrual symptoms as women—lethargy, irritability, and belligerence. In another project, Dr. Janiger searched the Human Relations Area Files for anthropological evidence to determine if the premenstrual syndrome was shaped by cultural factors. Finding no such support, he and his assistants compiled a questionnaire and made a study of Lebanese, Apache, Japanese, Nigerian, Greek, and American girls. They found more similarities than differences among the individuals from these diverse cultures. The premenstrual syndrome seemed to be universal with consistent reports of abdominal bloating, irritability, nervousness, depression, fatigue, allergies, backache, and moodiness.

In her chapter dealing with the social significance of the premenstrual syndrome, Dalton concludes with the following statement:

> The social ramifications of these varied effects of the premenstrual syndrome range from the insignificant to the dangerously significant. They affect in a greater or lesser degree the success or failure, and the happiness or misery of a considerable section of humanity in all walks of life and at all ages. It is therefore important that all doctors and social workers should have a full understanding of this syndrome (p26).

Sex Differences in Mental Functions

One need not stop with animal experiments and studies of stress and homosexuality to find evidence of innate behavioral potential differences between men and women. Dr. Lewis M. Terman and his associates at Stanford University set out forty years ago to find a large group of children with exceptionally high I.Q.s. From the beginning Terman found that it was easier to locate very bright boys than very bright girls, and the disparity increased slightly with age. It has been suggested that his findings indicate that whatever I.Q. tests measure, boys maintain higher I.Q.s better than girls (Herrnstein, 1971). This despite the fact that most I.Q. tests have been designed to minimize sex differences.

Dr. Jerome Kagan (1969) of Harvard University recently noted that over a thousand different studies have been published on sex differences in mental functioning. He points out that although many different tests have been used, two findings consistently emerge. One, females consistently outperform males on any test of language skill. Not only do girls begin to talk earlier than boys, but they have higher reading scores and better memories for language. Two, boys consistently outperform girls on nonverbal spatial tasks. Noting that the usual explanation for such findings is that such behaviors are learned during the first few years of life (a point which, it might be added, many Women's Liberationists are most adamant about), Dr. Kagan decided to test the proposition. In his experiment, Dr. Kagan selected one hundred and sixty first-born, white infants from the Cambridge-Boston area. At ages four months, eight months, thirteen months, and twenty-seven months, they were shown pictures of human faces. Some of the pictures were of normal faces; others showed features that were radically rearranged, such as an eye on the forehead. In addition, at each session infants were given auditory stimuli in the form of short meaningful words and nonsense syllables from a speaker at the side of the baby's head. Notes were made of the infants' responses to the visual and auditory stimuli, including fixation on the stimuli, vocalization time in response to stimuli, changes in heart rate (it slows down when infants concentrate), smiling, and fretting.

Dr. Kagan found that girls were more consistent in their vocalization in response to both kinds of stimuli. Vocalization was highly correlated with attention to stimuli in girls but not so in boys. He also found that the tendency to vocalize was correlated with social class for girls but not for boys. In another research project, this time involving only six-month-old infants, Kagan and an associate (1969) found that girls vocalized significantly more to faces than to geometric forms, whereas boys vocalized equally to both kinds of stimuli. Dr. Kagan notes that several other experiments by other investigators revealed similar results. Kagan offers two possible explanations for such findings. Well-educated mothers, Kagan found, engage in more face-to-face vocalization with daughters than poorly educated mothers; but he found no class differences in mothers' responses to male children. Thus, the results can be interpreted as being due to social factors. (It is interesting to note that rhesus monkey mothers treat male and female offspring differently.) As an alternative explanation, Dr. Kagan suggests that the left hemisphere of the brain, the side most involved in speech in most individuals, develops faster and is more specialized for language in girls. Boys, on the other hand, are less specialized for speech but the right side of the brain is more specialized for nonverbal activities.

In regard to the second explanation, Dr. Kagan notes a research project by Dr. Herbert Lansdell (1968). Dr. Lansdell found that when the cortex is removed from either side of the brain, removal of gray matter from the left disrupts functioning of language in females more than males, whereas removal of material from the right side disrupts the nonverbal activities in males more than females. Kagan also notes that investigation into right-ear, left-ear dominance in the ability to process language information revealed right-ear dominance for both boys and girls at the age of three, with girls exhibiting right-ear, left hemisphere dominance at age five and boys' scores indicating less clear dominance. Left-hemisphere advantage was found to hold only for language, however, and not for non-linguistic sounds.

Additional studies have revealed other nonlanguage differences between male and female infants. Newborn females have been found to react more to removal of a covering blanket and are more sensitive to air-jet stimulation of the abdomen than newborn males (Bell and Costello, 1964). Newborn females have a significantly higher basal skin conductance than newborn males (Weller and Bell, 1965); newborn males raise their heads higher than newborn females (Bell and Darling, 1965).

Clearly, there is some evidence that males and females differ in the rate of development of certain parts of the brain. They also appear to differ in the degree to which certain parts of the brain become specialized for certain tasks, such as language and spatial perception.

In summary, then, there is mounting evidence that suggests that there are real and significant differences between males and females both in the construction and development of the central nervous system and in the behavior that the nervous system initiates. Among Women's Liberationists, the validity of such evidence will be admitted grudgingly, if at all. Certainly, though, these differences should be taken into account by reasonable persons who propose and evaluate future programs of social change.

4

How False The Argument

—Dante

A great many American men are not accustomed to
doing monotonous repetitive work which never ushers
in any lasting let alone important achievement. This is
why they would rather repair a cabinet than wash
dishes. (Pat Mainardi, "Politics of Housework" from
Sisterhood Is Powerful, Robin Morgan (ed.), 1970, p.
451)

Women's Liberationists have failed to understand the ways
in which this society has favored women through laws and
customs.

According to the rhetoric, women in America are exploited
both financially and sexually, and are systematically
prevented from fulfilling themselves personally and
professionally. Further, Women's Liberationists claim that
these practices relegate them to second-class citizens, comparable to racial and ethnic minority groups.

I believe that an objective analysis of the life style of most
American women reveals that Women's Liberationists have
not only misanalyzed the role of the males in American
society, but they have also grossly underestimated the quality
of life of the American female. I believe that, far from being
patriarchal and male-dominated, American society, if not in
name is in practice, semi-matriarchal.

Many observers of American history have commented on the privileged status and life style that American women, in general, enjoy. Alexis de Tocqueville and Mark Twain are among the commentators. Both observed the pride that American men took in their efforts to make the lives of their wives and daughters as comfortable as possible, and both noted that American men were especially proud of the relative status American women enjoyed compared to their European counterparts.

Historical View

In order to understand the somewhat privileged position afforded women in American society it is necessary to turn to our history. American culture flows, for the most part, from a line that can be traced from the ancient civilizations of the Middle East, through Greece and Rome, to France and England and eventually to the North American continent. In Greece and Rome, women were awarded no special status. Even Aristotle wrote on their inferiority (*Natural History*, IX, I. *Politics*, I, 2).

Women's privilged status in our society is to a great extent attributable to the idealization of the phenomena of romantic love. Romantic love, the intense emotional experience involving the idealization and virtual worship of the qualities of a member of the opposite sex, while undoubtedly present in these early civilizations, was, as in most of the societies of the world, not emphasized. As the late Dr. Ralph Linton (1936), a prominent anthropologist, has noted, most societies regard individuals who have had the bad luck of "falling in love". . . as unfortunate and point out the victims of such attachments as horrible examples." In such societies, romantic preferences are not important in sexual and marital choices; like the modern Navajo Indians of the Southwest today, one woman is regarded as much like another—economic status and capacity for work and cooperation are the most important criteria for marriage. Romantic attachments are too diaphanous and relations are contracted on the basis of personal willingness in accordance with cultural rules and regulations regarding proper time, place, and person and not romance per se.

During the Middle Ages in Western Europe (particularly France) our habit of idealizing and pampering women got its start. It began in the castles and royal courts where there was a scarcity of well-bred ladies and an over-abundance of bachelor knights and troubadours. Because she was noble and had little to do but be charming and well-groomed; because the line between nobility and godliness was blurred; and because Christianity was fixated on the Madonna, the royal lady became the embodiment of beauty and purity to the many men who served her. Troubadours composed and sang ballads in the name of their lady love and knights wore their love's handkerchiefs and scarfs in jousts and did battle in their lady's name. Although frequently the lady was married, usually to the lord or other nobility of the castle, proclamations of love from knights and troubadours caused no problem because love and marriage and love and sex were believed to be incompatible. Sexual favors for the bachelor lovers were provided by the peasant women of the village; thus the purity of the knight's relationship with his lady was preserved; the closest he came to carnal knowledge of her was the apparently common practice of ritually undressing her and putting her to bed.

Ira Reiss (1960, p. 56), in his discussion of the history of romantic love, or courtly love as it should be called, believes that the Normans brought the custom with them in their invasion of England in the eleventh century. Though the idealistic denial of sexual relations between lady and her "lover" lasted for several centuries, by the sixteenth century lovers' deeds began to be rewarded by carnal favors. By the middle of the sixteenth century extra-marital coitus was an expected and formalized part of the love relationship. Since lower classes when possible almost always emulate the customs and status symbols of the higher classes, the love practices of the nobility began to filter down to the peasant classes. Soon it was the tendency to regard all women, regardless of their wealth, as little less than ladies of the royal court. The image of a woman was that of goodness and purity. She was to be treated as royalty and worshipped in the stylized custom of romantic or courtly love.

Our European ancestors brought this romanticized view of women with them to America. The style of life adopted by the immigrants in the New World did not dispel this system of practices and beliefs.

On the frontier, women were scarce, and when a woman was present in a community, either as a prostitute or as a part of a family, she was held in high regard by men starved for sex and feminine company. Consequently women were pampered and treated with respect as much as possible under the circumstances. The custom of men treating women in a romantic and concerned manner has carried down through the last several generations and currently finds expression in such things as a man's desire to provide a modern and convenient home for his wife, manners showing deference to women, control of the consumer economy by women, protective legislation for women (such as labor laws and laws against statutory rape), greater value of life insurance policies held by men, and cosmetic and fashion industries catering to the beautification of women rather than men.

Male vs Female Health

It is common to evaluate the standard of living and quality of life of a group by examining the health of its members. Life expectancy figures are known to be particularly revealing. In general, exploited groups exhibit life expectancies substantially below that of more privileged groups within the same society. In terms of life expectancy, the American white female enjoys, according to the latest edition of the

Demographic Yearbook of the United Nations, 7.4 years greater life expectancy at birth than her American male counterpart. The newborn nonwhite female also enjoys 7.4 years greater life expectancy than newborn nonwhite males, although the nonwhite female's life expectancy is 7.4 years shorter than her white American counterpart. According to the figures presented in the *Demographic Yearbook,* in only three countries of the world is the life expectancy differential between male and female newborns greater than it is in the United States. In Gabon in West Africa, there is a twenty-year differential; males have a life expectancy at birth of 25 years and females 45 years. In the Ryukyu Islands (which include Okinawa), the differential is 7.6 years, and in France the difference is 7.5 years.

In seven European countries, England, Denmark, France, Iceland, Netherlands, Norway, and Sweden, newborn females can expect to live longer than newborn American females. The differentials in life expectancy that these European females enjoy over their respective male counterparts range from a low of 4.5 years in Denmark to a high of 7.5 years in France. The average differential for the seven European countries is 5.7 years. Put another way, the average differential between male and female life expectancy in seven industrially and medically advanced countries in Europe is 1.7 years shorter than the differential between American men and women. As previously noted, women are probably at a genetic advantage in relation to males when it comes to resistance to disease. Thus, except under the most primitive conditions, especially where the hazards of childbirth are not controlled, one would expect women to live longer than men. On a world wide basis this is generally true because women have a shorter life expectancy than men in only a very few countries such as India and Pakistan. The question is, How much longer should a woman live than a man? How much of the differential in life expectancy between man and women in America is due to genetics and how much is due to social factors? The data from the advanced European countries suggest that women, under present medical technology, are programmed to live about five years longer than males. Deviation from this figure is an indication of some sort of medical or social advantage or disadvantage of the particular sex. Thus the fact that American women exceed the European average by more than a year and a half suggests that American women have a privileged status. (Privilege is measured in terms of 1.5 years longer life.)

There is other medical evidence for woman's privileged status in America. Between 1900 and 1950, the death rate for both sexes and all age groups was clearly down (Klebba, 1971). In the late 1950s there was a sudden change. While the death rates for women either leveled off or continued downward, there was a dramatic upturn in the mortality of males for all races. Latest available data indicate this trend is still continuing. Such an upturn in male mortality can be seen as continuation of the exaggeration of the differential in male-female life expectancies. In 1910, for example, there were 106 men for every 100 women, now there are but 95 men for every 100 women. With such a dramatic reduction in numbers, if human males were a species of wildlife, conservationists would begin to show concern for their survival. If this process is not reversed in the next hundred or so years, human males of the American society will have to be placed on "the endangered species" list.

During the last fifteen years there has been an upturn among younger men in deaths from suicide, homicide, motor vehicle accidents, cirrhosis of the liver, and lung cancer. Among older men, death rates from cancer (especially lung cancer), motor vehicle accidents, cirrhosis of the liver, emphysema, heart disease, and stroke are up. While deaths from heart attack among men outnumber women nearly two to one, there is every indication that as women join men in the stress-filled jobs, women's rates are increasing. During the last seven years, for example, heart disease deaths among women under age forty-five were up 11 percent.

The relationship between cigarette smoking and lung cancer, not to mention heart disease, is well known. Forty years ago cigarette smoking was primarily a male habit and consequently lung cancer was largely a male disease. Woman's desire for "independence" has necessitated the creation of symbols of independence. Unfortunately the cigarette is one such symbol. Smoking is now projected as a symbol of female independence and more women smoke than ever. Rates of lung cancer among women are also up.

Jurisprudence

Statistics dealing with crime are so biased against males that frequently data are not broken down according to sex. However, the statistics that are available seem to indicate that innate behavioral differences between the sexes and the nature of our society drive men to commit more crimes. In 1969, 86 percent of all persons arrested were male (*Statistical Abstract*, 1971, p. 146). Male homicides outnumber female homicides more than three to one (*Abstract*, 1971, p. 142). Of the 220,932 persons admitted into federal and state prisons in 1967, all but 6,947 were male (*Abstract*, 1971, p. 155).

However, as women strive for and achieve a life style that is more like men, their crime rate increases. Between 1960 and 1969, for example, the rate of charges against females for serious crimes increased 156 percent; for males it increased 61 percent. In larceny cases, there was a 196 percent increase in charges against females and a 62 percent increase against males. In offenses against family and children, charges against females increased 13 percent, but against males decreased 5 percent (*Abstract*, 1971, p. 146).

Males are most frequently the victims of crime. In a study based on a nation-wide survey of 10,000 households, males outnumber females as victims of crime nearly three to one for all age groups. In no age group was the frequency of female victims higher than males (*Abstract,* 1971, p. 143).

I have kept an informal count of the conviction of murderers in the state of Colorado over the last two decades. Males, especially minority group members, consistently receive heavy sentences for such crimes as killing their wives, while women frequently receive light sentences or no sentence at all for killing their husbands. Often the plea is, "I was forced to kill him because he was drunk and abusing me." When a woman is convicted of a crime, the blame is frequently placed on a man: "Some bastard who led the poor innocent thing down the road of ruin." Prisons are filled with men who have been convicted of "rape." Many are serving time for statutory rape; that is, having carnal knowledge not necessarily sexual intercourse, with an underaged female. In most states, the age of consent is eighteen, reflecting our attitude about the innocence and purity of women. We attempt to prolong the period of innocence well beyond the period of physiological or psychological capability. Many societies, including the English and the Navajo Indians, consider it appropriate for a young lady to have sexual relations with an older man shortly after puberty. To further illustrate how the double standard operates, imagine how foolish an underaged male would look if he tried to press charges of statutory rape against an older woman.

Deference to Women

In family matters, the American male is also at a severe legal disadvantage. The father is most often legally required to support the mother and children. In many instances, it is the father, and not the mother, who is responsible for the children well beyond their age of consent. It is rare indeed for a wealthy female to be required to pay alimony to a male in order that he may continue to live in a manner to which he has become accustomed. Yet, as is well known, it is quite common for a man to make heavy alimony payments to childless former wives even if the payments contribute to the deprivation of her former husband's second family. Fathers usually make child support payments when the children reside with the mother, but the mother rarely makes payments to the father when he has custody. Most lawyers and courts automatically assume that the mother will have primary custody rights; the father receives only visitation privileges. Further, a divorced woman is considered by most courts to be an adequate family for a child, but a divorced male somehow is inadequate. In addition, in most courts it is relatively easy to prove a man an unfit father, yet it is difficult to prove even the worst woman an unfit mother. Few would argue that in matters such as these, women receive considerable preferential treatment before the law.

Women also receive considerable deference according to custom. A gentleman opens doors for a lady, lights her cigarette, speaks politely and never argues vigorously with her, especially in public. Recently in the Southwest an adult male was sentenced to a jail term for using foul language in the presence of women. When men can afford it, they cater to a woman's desire to buy nice clothes, go to beauty parlors, decorate their home. A man constantly finds himself adjusting to a woman's often violent fluctuations in mood — due no doubt in large part to the action of hormones. Around the house when there is "heavy work" to be done, most men find that it has been left to them, while the women restrict themselves to the "feminine tasks" more suited to their "delicate nature." Even most toilet seats in most homes are designed for the female anatomy, the nearly round hole decidedly discriminating against the protruding male organ.

Women as Sex Objects

Women's Liberationists frequently complain of sexual exploitation by men. The prostitute is often cited as a particularly blatant and vicious example of male sexual exploitation of women. For those who have studied the phenomena of prostitution, this is at best a half truth. In the first place prostitution exists because of the scarcity of sex and female companionship among certain male groups. While it is true that the institution of prostitution is often demeaning to women, it is also true that one of the primary elements of the prostitute-"trick" relationship is for the prostitute to strip her "customer" of his money. Her intention is to provide as little service as possible in return for as much money as she can get. Prostitutes scheme, plan, and develop highly sophisticated techniques for "hustling" to relieve each "trick" of as much of his resources as possible. Further, it should be mentioned that at least in America there are other avenues of employment open to women besides prostitution. Most prostitutes stay in the racket by their own choice; they stay because of the pay, which is much higher than could possibly be hoped for in any other profession. Salaries much higher, I might add, than available in the Women's Liberationists' much aspired to college professorships.

Many women also frequently complain of the human male's seemingly universal habit of "leering" at women and pictures of nude women. Many women, and some men, find this trait repulsive and label it perversion. This, however, is not the case. Once again we must look to evolution for an explanation for this behavior. In no society in the world do the women go about everyday life with their genital areas uncovered. There are, however, a number of societies where penises are frequently unclothed. The human male finds the sight of the human female's external genital organs (excluding the breast) so sexually exciting that if women did not keep their pubic areas covered, the social unrest engendered by attacks on women would be so disruptive that the society would perish.

The existence of the male's passion for the sight of the female hips and genitals again lies in the biological transformation that took place long ago: the transition from a mother/child-centered family to a father/mother-centered family. Subhuman primate males do not exhibit a powerful response to the sight of a female's genital organs. In fact among many species of primates, a common social gesture of friendliness involves the female's presenting her hindquarters to the face of the male. The human male's passion for a view of the female's genitals and hips stems from the development of continuous sexual receptivity on the part of the female and the evolutionary need for the male to take a continuous sexual interest in the family relationship. Evolutionally, this was accomplished by providing the male with an insatiable need to view and touch her hips and sex organs. In this situation, if a male's eye begins to wander a bit, all a female usually has to do is provide him with the sight of her unclothed genitals, and providing another female hasn't done the same, he is stuck to her like glue. The mechanism for this tropistic behavior, although more sophisticated, is probably not unlike that of the frog; if a small black object crosses its visual field, its tongue automatically darts out and snares the object. The frog does not think about catching the fly; it is a reflex-like response.

In the adult human male, the mere sight of the female genitals elicits a nearly automatic response. There is also some evidence from research with monkeys which indicates the females secrete a substance from the labia area of the genitals which serves as an olfactory attraction to males. Olfactory experience may be below the threshold of consciousness. It has been suggested that this same mechanism is also at work in human beings. This conceivably accounts for tremendous sex appeal in women who are not necessarily beautiful or even unusually attractive. Whereas some beautiful women have no appeal whatsoever.

Insofar as an adult sexual relationship is concerned, there is no exploitation if the relationship is natural and enjoyable. If it is not enjoyable, then perhaps one has the wrong person. If it is still not enjoyable, perhaps one has the wrong sex. If it is still not, then perhaps one has the wrong species, or perhaps one works best alone or perhaps one is really asexual and should not be doing it in any form in the first place—there are plenty of options. If one gets pleasure, how can one be exploited?

The Women's Liberation movement has clearly distorted the position of the American woman. But their rhetoric apparently has wide appeal. Why is their view being accepted by so many?

Throughout history, when social systems begin to change and degenerate through internal upheaval, it is necessary for the members of the society to develop a rationalization—some more or less systematic explanation—for what is taking place. It does not really matter whether the explanation they adopt is sound or valid as long as it is psychologically satisfying to people who are going through the social transition. Studies of nativistic movements, for example, demonstrate that when a people need a rationalization for their experiences, they are apt to seize and further elaborate upon any explanation that happens to be about.

An example is the use of Marxist philosophy. Marxist ideology, emphasizing the organization of the workers and inculcating hostility toward the capitalist, dangles the ideological carrot of "freedom" before the "workers" at a critical time in the history of a nation and serves the social function of organizing the workers into needed collectives. The collective, organized and staffed by the workers, serves the employer's interests by organizing and placing skilled labor at the employer's immediate disposal. While Marxist ideology was directed against the employer, it also served to protect the industrial class from any upward social movement of the radical workers, since its revolutionizing process makes the worker hostile to the very idea of ownership. Becoming a Marxist revolutionary was then and is now tantamount to taking poverty vows and virtually assures life-long service as an employee.

Another example can be seen in the breakup of the extended family in the early part of this century in the United States and the sudden popularity of Freudian theory and its subsequent extensive use by the psychiatric profession. During a period in which the extended family (mother, father, children, and grandparents) was breaking up, Freudian theory, administered to the well-to-do by psychiatrists and to the common man through the popular press, served the function of relieving an adult individual of guilt when he was forced to, in one way or another, abandon his parents. When people's aged mothers and fathers are left to fend for themselves or are sent to old folks' homes, their adult children were in effect told they need not feel bad about it. Freudian theory and the stress on oedipal and electra complexes served as a subtle rationalization: one should not be living with one's parents in the first place.

At a period in the evolution of American society when the nuclear family (mother, father, and unmarried children) is under severe stress, Women's Liberation serves the same function as the Freudian theory did a couple of generations earlier. The dogma of exploitation and servitude provides women and men with a rationalization for women leaving the security of the home, sending the children off to day care centers, and entering the cold, impersonal, and frequently meaningless world of the wage earner. Men and women who have been forced to sell their services on the labor market already know that most wage work soon becomes drudgery. They are under no illusions because work has been a part of their lives; they know it is a struggle whose only reward, frequently as not, is mere survival at something less than an optimal level. That is why the Women's Liberation movement has found so few advocates among lower-class, middle-aged women who have worked most of their lives. Such women know firsthand that most jobs are boring. Yet many young, upper-middle-class women, sheltered from reality most of their lives, do not know this, and so the dogma, rhetoric, and glamour of the movement helps provide the psychological basis for breaking with tradition.

5

Appearances are Deceiving

—Aesop

Perhaps the most serious charge that can be leveled at the Women's Liberation movement is that it is reactionary. Far from being a progressive instrument in the humanization of society, it is in fact a serious impediment to the attempt of all citizens, of both sexes and of all races and ethnic groups, to build a better society.

Opposition from Blacks

Black people, who, in recent history, have had the most experience fighting for their rights, seem to instinctively know this. Black women are simply not buying what Women's Liberationists are selling. In an article dealing with Women's Liberation on the college campuses, Janice Law Trecker (*Saturday Review,* October 16, 1971) noted, for instance, that opposition to Women's Liberation from the blacks on the campuses is common; many blacks believe that women's studies are a ploy to attract attention away from the real problems of minorities. In an article in *Science* (of all places) on the state of Women's Liberation within the Department of Health, Education, and Welfare in the federal government, Judy Chase (1971) quotes one black employee as saying, "You don't have a heavy concentration of blacks involved in women's action because they feel that they have to deal with their own blackness first. Some say, 'Hell, what good is this for me? Let me get up where they (white women) are; first."

Middle-Class Rip-Off

If Women's Liberationists have their way, upper-middle-class white women will have all the high echelon jobs and prestigious positions, leaving the lower, less desirable positions to the lower yet-to-be-liberated poor women of all races. This seems inevitable since white upper-middle-class women are the only ones who are currently qualified in large numbers for the higher positions. They have had the educational privileges which are part of membership in the upper middle class. Women's Liberationists do not concern themselves with minority women's rights or the problems of poor people in general. They want the best jobs. An examination of the rhetoric of Women's Liberation now taking place within HEW (U.S. Department of Health, Education, and Welfare) clearly reveals this middle-class ethnocentrism. According to the article by Miss Chase, one of the major complaints in HEW is that 89 percent of the women employed in HEW hold jobs of GS-9 (Government Service) and below. Further, only 4 individuals out of 75 employees with grade 17 civil service ratings are women, and no women are numbered among the 19 persons with GS-18 ratings. Of the top 21 executives in HEW, only one is a woman. Miss Chase goes on to point out that the female ratio in grades 11 to 18 is considerably lower than 50-50 which one would "reasonably expect." She also notes the complaint that in the Food and Drug Administration none of the top 90 managers are women. Never mind the fact that only 7.5 percent of Ph.D. scientists and only 7 percent of all physicians are women. This is beside the point when one's expectations exceed his qualifications. It is interesting to note that the pay range in government service for a GS-9 is between $10,470 and $13,611 per year; for a GS-13 the range is $17,761 to $23,089 per year; and for a GS-17, it is $32,546 to $36,886 per year.

While the women at HEW complain about who is going to make between $17 and $23 thousand a year and who is going to make between $32 and $36 thousand a year, 50 percent of the American Indian families in this country live on cash incomes below $2 thousand per year and 75 percent live on incomes below $3 thousand. While middle-class white women in Washington squabble about who is going to get the cream of the bureaucratic jobs, 52 percent of the rural Spanish surnamed families in the Southwest and 31 percent of urban Spanish surnamed families earned less than $3 thousand a year. In 1970, 25.5 million Americans lived in poverty — 17.5 million whites and 8 million members of minority groups; the total number of poor actually increased by 1.2 million between 1969 and 1970. Yet nothing is heard from the Women's Liberationists on these problems; they are virtually silent on all subjects except their own supposed exploitation. Exploitation is defined as GS-9 position paying as much as $13 thousand a year rather than a GS-17 which pays as much as $36 thousand a year. From people with their educational background, we might expect a more macroscopic view of American social problems.

Fundamental Reform

Women's Liberationists' emphasis on more equitable distribution of jobs between the sexes is still another good example of the reactionary character of the movement. Rather than speak of a major reform in our social system which might involve such things as guaranteed income, productive · work for all able-bodied citizens, alternative forms of more equitable distribution of wealth, elimination of work through the elimination of useless and duplicative positions, increased utilization of automation and technology to take people out of assembly line work, Women's Liberationists emphasize the redistribution of existing jobs and have thereby further reinforced an economic system that is in deep trouble. Rather than speed the day when technological and economic changes might better the lives of all people, Women's Liberationists seem to be content to patch up the existing system by furthering their own economic gain.

Diverts Attention

Further, the Women's Liberationists' penchant for creating ferment and gaining publicity only serves as a smoke screen and attention-getting device from the real problems of this country: poverty, minority rights, crime, pollution, war, and the lack of national purpose. TV time and newspaper and magazine space are limited. The average citizen's capacity to deal with problems is limited; he can only cope with one or two at a time. To the same extent that the media and the average citizen are occupied with Women's Liberation they exclude from their consideration the real problems of the nation. The involvement of women in the pseudo-radical movement of their liberation takes them away from involvement in problems in which their real self-interest lies. Women's Liberation diverts attention from the valid possibilities of change. Thus, it is in the interest of all concerned people to see Women's Liberation for what it is — a reactionary child of the middle class. Whether deliberate or not, its effect will be not only to alienate the sexes, but to contribute to the further preservation of a social order whose reform is long overdue. If a justification for the breakup of the nuclear family must be found and some sort of rationale for technology's usurpation of women's functions in the home be evolved, let it not be one that is ignorant in its analysis and reactionary in its effects. Let it not be one that contributes further to the predicament of the poor.

What Price Freedom?

There is yet another sense in which the Women's Liberation movement is reactionary. In this case, reactionary is not used in the negative sense, but only to indicate a return to the past. Erich Fromm pointed out years ago that freedom can be quite burdensome for the individual; many choices are frequently worse than no choice. Like Byron's "Prisoner of Chillon" we all seem to long for freedom's choices only to eschew them when they come. The decade that spanned the turbulent years between the late 1950s and the late 1960s brought a revolution in sexual attitudes and to some extent behavior in the United States and other Western countries. Because of changes in attitudes, women, especially younger unmarried ones, became more free to engage in sexual relations without fear of the social stigma which used to be associated with such female behavior.

The young women did not attain this new freedom without paying a price, however. The least important of the negative effects of this new freedom was epidemic-like increases in venereal disease. In a pre-antibiotic age this epidemic would have been a catastrophe. There is some evidence that our stringent puritanical sex code can be traced to widespread incidence of venereal disease in England during the seventeenth century and the well-known developmental effects which presence of the disease in the mother has on the offspring. A religious belief grew out of a folk observation that those girls who "play around" tend to have malformed babies.

Of greater importance is the fact that in making themselves easily available to men women cheapened the market value of the one thing they have that men cannot do without, or at least don't like to; namely, the giving of themselves physically. By making herself easily available sexually to men, a woman placed herself on a par with other women. Such a woman has little to offer a man that he could not get from another woman. By making sex cheap and easy, women gave up their trump card; they sacrificed the one thing guaranteed by evolution to hold a man—the sight and use of her genitals (see Chapter 4). Mother Nature has put a rider on the guarantee, however. The sight and use of a woman's genitals works on the promiscuous male only in a market of scarcity. If the sight and use of the genitals of other women are readily available, no woman can expect to hold her man's attention indefinitely.

There is still a third problem that the new promiscuity has engendered. Because of the human female's ancient drives and primate heritage, indeed her animal heritage, the most important order of business in the life of a woman is to attract a male, establish something analogous to a nest, within the limitations of her society, begin reproduction, and provide for the continuance of her species. From a biological and evolutionary point of view, these needs constitute the indisputable foundation of the purpose of her life. The motto of a woman's existence is "born to give life." The impermanence of countless affairs, the rudderless drift from one "shack-up" to the next, the emptiness of being barren are alien to her character. But it is this alien state that the new sexual freedom presupposes. As a consequence many modern women find themselves fleeing from this freedom.

Clothed in the fabric of political rhetoric, the Women's Liberation movement can be seen as such a flight. As Midge Decter (*The Atlantic Monthly,* August, 1972) has pointed out, talk of the primacy, indeed the exclusivity of the clitoral orgasm, of homosexuality as a valid alternative to heterosexuality, of celibacy and sexual exploitation is but a symbolic plea for chastity. A clitoral orgasm is achieved by external manipulation and need not involve male penetration; lives of homosexuality or celibacy are conducted without males; a discussion of sexual exploitation is merely a plea for no sex. From this point of view, Women's Liberation is a desire on the part of the modern female to return to the past when there were no real sexual choices and all decent women remained chaste until marriage and then faithful to their husbands. Women's Liberation is a weird effort on the part of modern women to be free of the freedoms of sexual inadequacy and worries of orgasm, to be free of the freedom to contract VD, to be free of the freedom to give away one's sexual bargaining power, to be free of the freedom that has led many to stray from the ancient path.

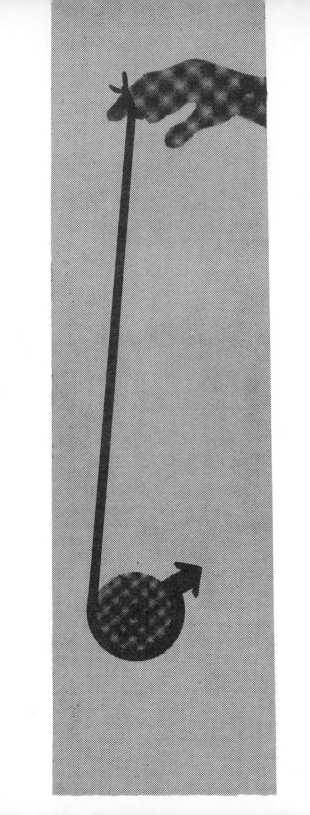

6

Hold Your Tongue and Let Me Love

—Donne

Several generations ago linguists discovered that the use of
words is absolutely vital to much of abstract human thought.
It is impossible, it was found, to engage in some forms of
thought without words. The problem is that words are not
objective. There is no one-to-one relationship between a word
and the thing in the world to which the word refers. Reality
can be sliced into an infinite variety of shapes with words. At
any given time in any given language or dialect, no two social
groups ever slice reality in quite the same way. Because of this
and because words condition the perception of reality, no two
groups perceive reality in quite the same way. But this does
not mean (and this is a commonly held fallacy in liberal
quarters) that an objective reality does not exist. It further
does not suggest that there are not techniques for the
objective study of that reality. At rock bottom this is what
science is all about—the objective study of reality.

But words do condition perception and perceptions influence behavior. Thus, an understanding of the manner in
which groups use certain words leads us to a greater
understanding of the group's behavior. Studies in social
change have noted that one of the first things that a social
group does in attempting to change its behavior is to change
the meaning of many of the words the group uses. Through

such changes it is often possible to change the members' perceptions and consequently modify their behavior. An excellent example of this phenomena is the distaste that many Women's Liberationists currently show for the use of certain terms that connote sex and role. The word *chairman* is one example. It is becoming more and more fashionable for liberated women and their liberal male supporters to refer to an individual serving in the capacity of chairman as *chairperson*. Women's Liberationists contend that use of the term *chairman* is discriminatory, because it is a noxious vestige from a period of history when women were subordinate to men in most aspects of life. Use of the word *chairperson*, they contend, is more dignifying, asexual, and reflects their new-found liberated status. Another neologism that Women's Liberationists frequently insist on using is *sexist*. For a man or even a woman to be labeled *sexist* is, judging by its use, a devastating insult.

A third term with similar pejorative connotations is the compound *male chauvinist*. The label of *male chauvinist* indicates a half-wit and a low-life. Within Women's Liberation, the use of these and other terms has taken on an air of magic. They are attempting to make the world more to their own liking by redefining it. While such linguistic gymnastics might help group solidarity and provide a vocabulary for hostility and negative feelings—particularly against males—it does little to change reality.

Further, such trivial tinkerings with the English language become ludicrous when one examines the historical derivations of many of the hated terms. The implications of such tamperings are rather interesting and humorous.

The word *chair* is derived from the French, meaning *pulpit* or *throne*. The word *man* is derived from the old English and originally meant *human being* or more accurately *one who thinks*. The word *chairman* is obviously a compound of *chair* and *man* meaning literally *one who thinks, who occupies the throne*. The term *person* on the other hand, is derived from the Latin term *persona*, meaning *role* or *mask*. Thus, *chairperson* means literally *one who occupies the throne who wears a mask or plays a role.* I prefer the term that gives reference to *intelligence* rather than the form that refers to *role playing* or *masks.*

The term *sex* in English is derived from the Latin word *scare* meaning *to cut* or a *division.* A *sexist* then is literally *one who cuts* or a *divisionist.* If Women's Liberationists insist on dividing contemporary society into two camps, those for *amalgamation* and those for *division,* I'm afraid that I will have to side with the *divisionists.* I think they have more fun.

The term *chauvinism* can be traced back to a French soldier, Nicolas Chauvin of Rochefort, known for his demonstrative patriotism to the First Republic, the Empire, and Napoleon. What, pray tell, can be wrong with a bit of demonstrative pride in being a member of the male sex—a *male chauvinist?* Conversely, what can be wrong with demonstrative pride in being a female—in being feminine or a female chauvinist—especially in view of the fact that the word *feminine* is derived from Latin meaning *the sucked one* or the *breast feeder.*

Recently, terms that denote the sex of either the speaker or the referent have come under attack. In this country such protestations are known as *de-sexing the English language.* Pronouns such as *he, she, him*, and *her*, have particularly been singled out. One proposal is to substitute the neuter *it* for traditional sexist pronouns. A second proposal, in a letter to *Ms.* Magazine (July, 1972, p. 43), noted that the term *one* can term *one* and still maintain one's pride in *oneself.* (*Ms.* term *one* and still maintain one's pride in *oneself.* (*Ms.* questioned what term would be used in, "If the student studies hard, [one (?) he (?)] will succeed"?)

While these proposals are not too radical, in a letter, which we assume to be serious, to the *Newsletter of the American Anthropological Association* (June, 1972, p. 4), Robert B. Kaplan, who signed his letter only as "Director, University

Southern California," suggested that the pronouns denoting masculinity and femininity *he, him, she,* and *her,* be combined into the neologisms *shis,* and *shim,* and that *his, himself, her,* and *herself,* be neologized to *shim(s)* and *shimself.* From a feminist point of view, however, there is only one thing wrong with Kaplan's proposal: all the four terms that he proposes use terms formerly denoting the male sex as the basic building block of the new, supposedly sex-free term. Thus, *shis,* which is supposed to be the subjective for *he* and *she,* is really *him* with an *s* on it, and *shimself,* which is the new reflexive for *himself* and *herself,* is again a mere sexist amalgamation of *him, self,* and an *s.* Clearly no self-respecting Women's Liberationist could accept terms that are so biased in their composition, particularly in view of the fact that they have been proposed by a male.

Another interesting example of sex differences in language change uses is a recent study by a University of California linguist. She noted that as women become "emancipated" they adopt more of the swear words of men, but few men adopt characteristically female terms (*divine, chic*). (*Psychology Today*, August, 1972, p. 16)

It is interesting to speculate on what other linguistic changes might be forthcoming. The term *woman*, for instance, might be a strong candidate for revision or might even be discarded. The term *man* as we saw originally meant *one who thinks*, but the activists have found this offensive because it also connotes the *male of the human species*. Thus, if *chairman* is rejected on the grounds that it includes the term *man*, *woman* might also be rejected. Some might suggest that *woman* be shortened to *wo*. Thus there would be *man*, for male and *wo* for woman. This will surely not be acceptable since the *wo* of *woman* is derived from the Old English meaning *wife* (*woman* literally means *wife man*). The term *female* will probably be equally unacceptable since it is a compound of the term *male*. As already noted, the term *feminine* or even *fem* is out because it refers to breast feeding which is regarded by some liberated women as a demeaning activity. (The term *liberated* refers to the state of being free; the term *free* has a wide and ancient derivation meaning originally *beloved, friend,* or *to love.*) With all the traditional terms being excluded, the liberationists will have to invent a new term to designate the female sex. I would suggest something close in meaning to the words *power, force, independence,* or *don't take nothin' from nobody.*

We might also expect that all terms that have historically been used to designate the sexes might be discarded because of negative memories of subordination and exploitation by man. *Man, male, stud, masculine, female, women, wife,* and *spouse* will probably be delegated to the linguistic graveyard. In addition, I predict there will be a revolt against the use of obvious female names (Judy, Mary, and Elizabeth) and obvious male names (Frank, Roy, Arnold, Carl). Women's Liberationists will soon insist that these names are discriminatory and have detrimental effect on the psychological development of the child because they help provide a sexual identity that is no longer appropriate and was never valid. Neuter names, such as Chris, Robin, and Kim will become even more popular than they are now. It might also be expected, as the Women's Liberation movement grows, that there will be a demand for the abolition of all references to gender in all languages.

We shall probably witness the elimination of terms of reference and title based on sex, such as: mister, mistress, miss and ms. In their place, we might expect the substitution of a single term, such as *person.* After all, sex is only a matter of role. In Orwell's *1984,* the sex act itself was permitted, but there was every effort to eliminate other aspects of sex from society.

7

What Does A Woman Want?

—Freud

Whenever Americans are faced with a real or imagined social problem they have traditionally attempted to solve the problem in one of two ways. One, they indiscriminately spend large sums of money in an effort to reverse what are believed to be the causes of the problem and/or two, they attempt to pass a law against some noxious behavior that seems to lie at the root of the problem. When the problem is of minor importance, the laws are passed at the local level; if the problems are of major importance, a federal law is passed; and if things are truly catastrophic, then an aroused public will only be satisfied with a constitutional amendment.

The experience of the last two generations suggests that the liberal view that spending money can alleviate all social problems ("if only enough is spent") is at best a quarter truth. The failure of the many expensive programs designed to eliminate poverty is but one example of the ineffectiveness of this approach. While the success of laws designed to eliminate social problems seems more difficult to evaluate than results achieved by spending money, especially in regard to complex problems, an examination of the social effects of the constitutional amendments during the last 110 years suggests that the rate of success here is also something less than spectacular.

For example, the 1870 Constitutional amendment guaranteeing equal rights to both white and colored citizens went largely unnoticed until the mid-1950s when it was necessary for civil rights activists to take to the streets to demand new laws to provide the rights that the 1870 amendment had guaranteed in the first place. The prohibition amendment of 1919 is now recognized as a disaster, and a second amendment was passed in 1933 to repeal it. The suffrage amendment of 1920 was supposed to set things right for women by providing them with the vote. Apparently it has not. Women tell us they need still another amendment. The amendment of 1951 limiting a president to two terms of office was merely an effort by Republicans to unload after Roosevelt's four terms. The 1961 amendment giving the District of Columbia the right to vote is socially insignificant. The twenty-fifth amendment regarding presidential disability and succession, passed in 1967, has not yet been used. (Section Four of the twenty-fifth amendment makes mutiny against the President legal.) The amendment of 1964, barring the poll tax, is a qualified success, but it is a testimony to the failure of the 1870 civil rights amendment. The 1971 amendment lowering the voting age to 18 years also remains to be tested.

To follow these dubious precedents, the Women's Liberationists are now asking the American people to pass a 27th amendment to the Constitution. "Equality of rights under the law shall not be denied or abridged by the United States or by any State on account of sex." In October 1971 the amendment cleared the House of Representatives by a margin of 354-23 and in March 1972 it cleared the Senate by a vote of 84 to 8, with most of the opposition coming from Southern and Western senators. If it is ratified by 38 states in seven years it will become law. A number of state legislatures have already ratified it; Hawaii did so 30 minutes after passage by the Senate.

Of the many effects that the Equal Rights Amendment supporters believe it will have, Women's Liberationists are most excited about its economic implications. Since the new law will supposedly outlaw job discrimination on the basis of sex, members of the movement expect a windfall of good jobs. Women's economic status, it is believed, will be substantially improved. However there are only so many jobs in the economy—so many good ones and so many bad ones. These jobs are distributed among men and women, and since most men and women are members of a family unit, it makes little difference who in the family has the high-paying job and who has the low-paying one; all the money goes to the support of the economic unit—the family. In fact, it is probably better for the family if the male has the high-paying job because men do not take time off for pregnancy and they miss fewer working days per year because they are sick less (they are sick less, but die younger). From the viewpoint of the whole society, the problem is that if women get more of the good, high-paying jobs, then there will be fewer of them for men; thus, women might make more money, men less; but since most people's income goes to the family unit, the average family is economically no better off; they may be only a little worse off because of more lost job time by women.

The only women who will come out ahead economically (unless there is a general economic expansion which the amendment does not guarantee) are those who are not members of a family unit. The widespread view that the lot of women will improve when they get better jobs is a myth.

The fallacious higher-pay issue is a product of the biased view of the Women's Liberationists. Most Liberationists are unmarried, childless, and under thirty; they see the world only in their own terms. Women's Liberationists will take good jobs away from family men, and the wives of the men who have been deprived will have to live on less income than they would have otherwise. The children of those couples will have less, and there will be a general reduction of the quality of society.

The proposed amendment will have the effect of forbidding federal aid to all schools, both public and private, that discriminate in any way on the basis of sex. On the surface this sounds fair; but it also includes schools that cater exclusively to boys or exclusively to girls. Thus, a school with an all-male or all-female student body will not receive federal funds. Without federal funds, educational institutions cannot exist today. While coed schools may be more popular than sexually segregated schools, there are some people who still prefer sexual segregation. In a society based on free choice, they should have the right to choose such schools.

Another effect of the law will be to make illegal the state's requirement that a woman assume the last name of her husband upon marriage. The name that the married couple adopts will have to be decided by another means, perhaps a hyphenated amalgamation of the two last names of the couple (for example, Christianson-Murphy) or a name different from either partner's name. The first proposal is ridiculous because surnames would soon become unwieldy. If Miss Smith marries Mr. Jones, their surname would be Smith-Jones. Their offspring would have to combine his "double" name with his spouse's double name. Further, whose name should come first, groom's or bride's? Perhaps the decision will be made on the flip of a coin. The selection of an entirely new name by the couple will be opposed by many because family names are a means of tracing kinship; many people still take pride in their family names and would take a dim view of a law that forbids use of family names.

In addition, the Equal Rights Amendment would forbid discrimination on the basis of sex in regard to military service. Because of the amendment and the protests of Liberationists, military service academies are making provision for the admission of female cadets in the upcoming years. Females would be eligible for the draft. Separate facilities for men and women will have to be provided on military bases. Military expenses for construction would go up. The new Russian light cruisers now have the firepower of a United States heavy cruiser because the Russians have saved space onboard ship by having the seamen sleep in the same bunks in shifts rather than each man having his own bunk as on American ships. The space saved on Russian ships is used for increased armaments. Would American women demand private quarters on cruisers and submarines?

As noted in Chapter 4, women in this country are much better off, enjoy a higher standard of living, and have more personal freedoms and rights than the women of almost any nation of the world. The proposed constitutional amendment on women's rights will only jeopardize their present position if it does anything. But will the amendment do anything? That is the question. The fact of the matter is it probably will not. Like the amendments before it, it will have little effect on what people do and think. The idea that new laws can solve our problems stems from the mistaken idea that behavior and social convention flow from law ratl.er than law from behavior and convention. Of course there is an interaction between law and behavior, but primarily, attitudes, beliefs, and behaviors determined by old cultural practices determine the form of the laws. In terms of cause and effect, laws come primarily after the fact and not before. Women's Liberationists can ram laws through Congress and state legislatures till hell freezes over, but they cannot significantly change people's beliefs or actions.

We come now to the most important reason the Equal Rights Amendment should be defeated. During the last 100 years (but especially during the last 20), the concept of the law has changed from protector of the rights of the individual to protector of the rights of groups. The Bill of Rights does not make any mention of minority or special interest groups. The noun used in reference to the recipients of guarantees in the Bill of Rights is "people." However, beginning in 1865 with the Thirteenth Amendment, which abolished slavery, constitutional amendments have dealt increasingly with minority rights. The Fourteenth Amendment declared equal rights for white and colored citizens in 1870; the Nineteenth Amendment gave suffrage to women in 1920; the Twenty-Fourth Amendment barred poll taxes in federal elections in 1964. Now the proposed Twenty-Seventh Amendment would grant equal rights to women.

In addition to constitutional amendments, during this same period a plethora of federal, state, and local laws and numerous court decisions at all levels have affirmed and championed the rights of certain groups. While the rights of minorities certainly should not be neglected or in any way abridged, the focus of our legal system should not be in the rights of groups but of individuals. If the rights of all individuals are guaranteed, then guarantees to special interest groups become unnecessary. Our legal system should be constructed so as to be blind to the sex, race, ethnic background, or economic class of the individual. Admittedly this approach may be more difficult, but it will be better for all in the long run.

Already there are danger signs from the excess of concern for minority rights. Perhaps the most serious of these is the quota system. Special treatment of an individual on the basis of his membership in a minority group, regardless of how well intentioned, is anti-democratic. It is in sharp conflict with the principle of equal opportunity. Preferential quotas for minorities to correct inequalities in opportunity is nothing more than the reallocation of equities. Not only does it reinforce old hostilities and create new ones, it sets a dangerous precedent. Jewish people, for example, remember all too well how effectively quota systems can be used to deny rights. An individual's ability and his contribution to society should be the sole basis of his success. When government at any level becomes the champion of the rights of minorities, as it increasingly has done for racial, ethnic, and sex minorities, it becomes little more than the pawn of special interest groups. While the granting of privilege to certain vocal minorities might appear reasonable today, there is no guarantee that it will be so tomorrow when another minority catches the public eye and pleads its case. The existence of quotas and special rights for minorities opens the door for opportunists who serve only their own ends through the manipulation of quotas and the granting of special privilege.

Laws passed during the last few years to insure the civil rights of racial minorities have not had the effect of making our legal system less conscious of race; if anything it has made it more so. Efforts to assure equal rights for racial minorities have, through the use of quota systems and preferential treatment, contributed to reverse discrimination. There is little to suggest that the effects of the Equal Rights Amendment will be different. Rather than being less conscious of sex, we will become more aware of sex differences. The privileges incurred by women through the "equal" treatment will only have the effect of creating discrimination against males. The quality of democratic society is not improved by such table-turning.

All these points aside, even if the Equal Rights Amendment is passed, and if it did have a chance to work as intended, it will not work. There is a basic flaw in it; its provisions do not apply where the biological characteristics of the sexes are involved. While Women's Liberationists have assumed that there are few important biological differences between the sexes, research thus far indicates that there are many and that they are significant. Since these differences are so vital in their determination of human behavior, the proposed amendment will eventually be subject to many qualifications in interpretation.

8

Frankly, My Dear,
I Don't Give A Damn!
—Clark Gable as Rhett Butler

Every age has its heros and its villains, its champions, its losers. Those persons lucky enough to wear the mantle of "hero" and "champion" are the embodiment of the positive values of their societies, the personification of what is believed to be good in that society. A hero is the ideal toward which the young can strive, grist for the fantasy mill for those for whom it is too late to be anything but what they are. Villains and losers serve the opposite effect. The "villain" or "loser" is the embodiment of the negative values of the society, a living characterization of what the young should not be. Heros and champions and villains and losers reflect the life and times of a people and appear in many places in a society. They appear not only in real life, but also in the religion and oral literature of more primitive societies. In more advanced cultures, such as our own, these mirrors of society also appear in literature and in TV and film.

It has been said that we live in an age in which there are no heros. This is not true, strictly speaking. We live in an age of anti-heros. The male heros (and most heros have traditionally been male) of modern myth and film are small in stature, spectacled, high-voiced, incompetent, introverted, self-searching, frustrated, dependent, socially dominated, negativistic, and impotent. They bear a strange congruency to our society—once dynamic, but now rudderless, adrift on a sea of bureaucracy, indecision, and liberal platitudes. The modern hero is as ineffective as he is effeminate. He stands for the abrogation of masculine values in this society; he is symbolic of the decline and fall of the power and prestige of the white male in America. He is amusing in his ineptitude; he is clever in inarticulation; like the court jester, he entertains but he cannot inspire men and leaves women cold as the dead.

To find "old" values we must look back to another time—back to the thirties, forties, and fifties for heros and champions of film.

From the 1930s to 1950s, Clark Gable was the undisputed hero of masculine culture. He was to the American motion picture what Ernest Hemingway was to American literature. Of these qualities, Joan Crawford, who co-starred with him in a number of films, said the following: "Gable became the romantic—and perhaps real—paragon of masculinity that women seek in men—but seldom find. Yet men identified with Gable because he never flaunted his masculinity and because he was flesh and blood and not a synthetic symbol." (Essoe and Lee 1967) Male identification with Gable, in fact, was so strong that in 1935 when he appeared bare-chested on the screen, T-shirts when out of style overnight and many male underwear manufacturers went out of business.

There was a theme that ran through Clark Gable's films. He usually played the part of strong, independent, intelligent, but not cerebral individual who became romantically involved with a lovely young woman who was also intelligent, strong, and equally independent. (In these films, starlets such as Joan Crawford, Barbara Stanwyck, and Greer Garson frequently played opposite Gable.) The lady's independence, which threatened the romance, stemmed in part from the fact that she was pursuing her career. In the films, Gable alwas took a "no-nonsense" approach to his problems with the lady and eventually convinced her of the error of her ways. She willingly reformed herself, knowing in her heart that if it came to a choice, it was better to have a good man than a good job. Times have changed, though. Hollywood does not make that kind of film anymore. Gable died in 1959, some say from the effects of overexertion in performing his own stunts in his last film. No star, with the exception of perhaps Marlon Brando, is remotely capable of taking his place. Others who projected masculine images such as Humphrey Bogart are also gone. Positive portrayal of masculine culture and by implication feminine culture in those days, perhaps so much a reflection of the dynamism of American society, is out. It is gone—along with the society that spawned it. In its place is the saga of the anti-hero—the eunuch, the castrated. It is impossible to know how long we shall have to suffer through this phase of history. Perhaps the return to sounder traditions is near; then again, perhaps this madness is only beginning.

The diversity of sexes is one of the few things left on this planet that makes life worthwhile. In a world where once good food has been rendered tasteless and in some cases inedible, where it is virtually impossible to get a clean breath of air or a little peace and quiet not to mention privacy, where more and more people live in the same ticky-tacky houses, where people wear the same ready-made clothes and chortle at the same stupid TV programs, God save what little diversity there is left between the sexes. But it does not take an astute social observer to know that the idea of the unisex and the test tube baby is on the move. It may well be that its time has come. If it has, culture may well mask many of the innate differences between men and women. There is, after all, no "law" in the universe that says social movements on earth must be rational, and must be formulated in accordance with man's nature. The results of such changes should they come may not necessarily be good; new social forces will place more strain on man's already overstressed and overextended primate nature.

But I must say that it will be a pretty dull place if the slovenly, pants-wearing, combat-booted, genetic females of the unisex species ever become the universal style. It will be one heck of a world when the last square yard of open ground is covered over with asphalt, when all the world is one long Wilshire Boulevard, where there won't be a solitary proud and elegant lady with well-rounded hip and trim thigh to send a fellow's mind reeling and his soul soaring.

References

Abbot, Sidney, and Barbara Soal
1972   *Sappho Was a Right-On Woman: A Liberated View of Lesbianism* (Stein and Day, New York).

Aristotle
        Natural History, IX, 1. *Politics,* I, 2.

Beach, Frank A.
1947   "A Review of Physiological and Psychological Studies of Sexual Behavior in Mammals," *Psychological Reviews,* vol. 27, pp. 240-307.

Bell, R. Q., and Naomi S. Costello
1964   "Three Tests for Sex Differences in Tactile Sensitivity in the Newborn," *Biologia Neonatorum,* vol. 7, pp. 335-347.

Bell, R.Q., and Joan F. Darling
1965   "The Prone Head Reaction in the Human Newborn: Relationship with Sex and Tactile Sensitivity," *Child Development,* vol. 36, pp. 943-949.

Branchey, Laure, M. Branchey, and R. D. Nadler
1971   "The Influence of Sex Hormones on Brain Activity in Male and Female Rats" in *Influence of Hormones on the Nervous System,* D.H. Ford, ed. (S. Karger, N.Y.), pp. 334-340.

Chase, Judy
1971   "Inside HEW: Women Protest Sex Discrimination," *Science,* Oct. 15, vol. 174, pp. 270-274.

Childs, Barton
1965   "Genetic Origin of Some Sex Differences among Human Beings," *Pediatrics,* vol. 35, pp. 798-812.

145

Dalton, Katharina
1964   *The Premenstrual Syndrome* (Charles C. Thomas, Springfield, Ill.).

D'Andrade, Roy G.
1966   "Sex Differences and Cultural Institutions," in *The Development of Sex Differences*, Eleanor E. Maccoby, ed. (Stanford University Press, Stanford, Calif.).

Decter, Midge
1972   "Toward the New Chastity," *The Atlantic Monthly*, August, pp. 42-55.

Devereux, George
1961   "Two Types of Modal Personality Models," in *Studying Personality Cross-Culturally*, Bert Kaplan, ed. (Harper & Row, N.Y.), pp. 227-241.

Dobzhansky, Theodosius
1972   "Species of Drosophila," *Science*, vol. 177, pp. 664-669.

Dornbusch, Sanford M.
1966   "Afterword" in *The Development of Sex Differences*, Eleanor E. Maccoby, ed. (Stanford University Press, Stanford, Calif.). pp. 205-219.

Dorner, G. and J. Staudt
1968   "Structural Changes in the Preoptic Anterior Hypothalamic Area of the Male Rat, Following Neonatal Castration and Androgen Substitution," *Neuroendocrinology*, vol. 3, pp. 136-140.

Drellich, Marvin G. and Sheldon E. Waxenberg
1966   "Erotic and Affectional Components of Female Sexuality," in *Sexuality of Women: Scientific Proceedings of the Tenth Annual Spring Meeting of the American Academy of Psychoanalysis*, Jules E. Masserman, ed. (Grune and Stratton, New York), pp. 45-55.

Eisenberg, J. F.
1972   "The Relation between Ecology and Social Structure in Primates," *Science*, vol. 176, May 26, pp. 863-874.

Essoe, Gabe and Ray Lee
1967   *Gable: A Complete Gallery of His Screen Portraits* (Price, Stern, Sloan, Los Angeles).

Federman, Daniel D.
1971   "A New Look at Homosexuality" (editorial), *The New England Journal of Medicine*, vol. 285, pp. 1197-1198.

Gadpaille, Warren J.
1972   "Research into the Physiology of Maleness and Femaleness," *Archives General Psychiatry*, vol. 26, pp. 193-206.

Ginsberg, George L., William A. Frosch, and Theodore Shapiro
1972   "The New Impotence," *Archives General Psychiatry*, vol. 26, pp. 218-220.

Goy, Robert W.
1968   "Organizing Effects of Androgen on the Behavior of Rhesus Monkeys," in *Endocrinology and Human Behavior*, Richard P. Michael, ed. (Oxford University Press, New York), p. 12-31.

Greenway, John
1962   Lectures at the University of Colorado.

Hamburg, David A.
1969   "Sexual Differentiation and the Evolution of Aggressive Behavior in Primates," in *Environmental Influences on Genetic Expression: Biological and Behavioral Aspects of Sexual Differentiation*, Norman Kretchmer et al., eds. (U.S. Government Printing Office, Washington, D.C.).

Harlow, H. F. and M. K. Harlow
1962   "The heterosexual affectional system in monkeys," *American Psychologist*, vol. 17, pp. 1-9.

1965   "The Effect of Rearing Conditions on Behavior," in *Sex Research: New Developments*, J. Money, ed. (Holt, Rinehart, and Winston, New York), pp. 161-175.

Harris, Geoffrey W.
1964   "Sex Hormones, Brain Development, and Brain Function," *Endocrinology*, vol. 75, pp. 627-648.

Harris, Marvin
1971   *Culture, Man, and Nature: An Introduction to General Anthropology* (Crowell, New York), pp. 583-584.

Hemingway, Ernest
1938   *The Short Stories of Ernest Hemingway* (Random House, New York), pp. 183-184.

Herrnstein, Richard
1971   "I.Q.," *The Atlantic Monthly*, September.

Hyyppa, M.
1971   "Hypothalamic Monoamines and Pineal Dopamine During Sexual Differentiation of the Rat Brain," *Experientia*, vol. 27, pp. 336-337.

Jensen, Gordon D.
1969   "Environmental Influences on Sexual Differentiation," in *Environmental Influences on Genetic Expression: Biological and Behavioral Aspects of Sexual Differentiation,* Norman Kretchmer et al., (U.S. Government Printing Office, Washington, D.C.).

Kagan, Jerome
1969   "A Sexual Dimorphism in Vocal Behavior in Infants," in *Environmental Influences on Genetic Expression: Biological and Behavioral Aspects of Sexual Differentiation,* Norman Kretchmer et al., (U.S. Government Printing Office, Washington, D.C.).

Kahl, Joseph A.
1961   *The American Class Structure* (Holt, Rinehart and Winston, New York).

Kartzinel, R., D. H. Ford, and R. K. Rhines
1971   "Lysine Accumulation in the Protein-Containing Fraction of the Rat Brain: The Effect of Age, Sex, and Neonatal Castration," in *Influence of Hormones on the Nervous System*, D.H. Ford, ed., (S. Karger, N.Y.), pp. 296-305.

Klebba, Joan A.
1971   *Leading Components of Upturn in Mortality for Men-United States-1952-1967,* Department of Health, Education, and Welfare Publication No. (HSM) 72-1008 (Department of Health, Education, and Welfare, Rockville, Md.).

Kolodny, Robert C., William Masters, Julie Hendryx, and Gelson Toro
1971   "Plasma Testosterone and Semen Analysis in Male Homosexuals," *The New England Journal of Medicine,* vol. 285, pp. 1170-1174.

Ladonsky, W. and L. C. J. Gaziri
1970   "Brain Serotonin and Sexual Differentiation of the Nervous System," *Neuroendocrinology,* vol. 6, pp. 168-174.

Lansdell, Herbert
1968   "The Use of Factor Scores from the Wechsler-Bellevue Scale of Intelligence in Assessing Patients with Temporal Lobe Removals," *Cortex,* vol. 4, pp. 257-268.

Linton, Ralph
1936   *The Study of Man* (Appleton-Century-Crofts, New York).

Luce, Gay Gaer
1971   *Biological Rhythms in Human and Animal Physiology* (Dover Publications, New York). Formerly *Biological Rhythms in Psychiatry and Medicine,* Public Health Service Publication No. 2088, 1970.

MacLean, Paul D.
1965   "New findings relevant to the evolution of psychosexual functions in the brain," in *Sex Research: New Developments,* J. Money, ed. (Holt, Rinehart, and Winston, New York), pp. 197-218.

1966   "Studies on the Cerebral Representation of Certain Basic Sexual Functions" in *Brain and Behavior: The Brain and Gonadal Function* (Vol. III), Roger A. Gorski and Richard Whalen, eds. (University of California Press, Berkeley, Calif.), pp. 35-79.

Martini, Luciano
1969   "Physiology: Hormonal Influences on the Development of the Hypothalamus of the Rat," in *Environmental Influences on Genetic Expression: Biological and Behavioral Aspects of Sexual Differentiation*, Norman Kretchmer et al., eds. (U.S. Government Printing Office, Washington, D.C.).

Michaels, Richard H. and Kenneth D. Rogers
1971   "A Sex Difference in Immunologic Responsiveness," *Pediatrics*, vol. 47, pp. 120-122.

Millett, Kate
1971   *Sexual Politics* (Avon Books, New York).

Moguilevsky, J. A., C. Libertun, O. Schiaffini, and B. Szwarcfarb
1968   "Sexual Differences in Hypothalamic Metabolism," *Neuroendocrinology*, vol. 3, pp. 193-199.

Money, John
1968   "Influence of Hormones on Psychosexual Differentiation," *Medical Aspects of Human Sexuality*, November, pp. 32-42.

Morgan, Robin (ed.)
1970   *Sisterhood Is Powerful: An Anthology of Writings from the Women's Liberation Movement* (Vintage Books, New York).

Moos, Rudolf H., Bert S. Kopell, Frederick T. Melges, Irvin D. Yalom, Donald T. Lunde, Raymond B. Clayton, and David Hamburg
1969   "Fluctuations in Symptoms and Moods During the Menstrual Cycle," *Journal of Psychosomatic Research*, vol. 13, pp. 37-44.

Murdock, George Peter
1935   "Comparative Data on the Division of Labor By Sex," *Social Forces*, vol. 15, pp. 551-553.

1957   "World Ethnographic Sample," *American Anthropologist*, vol. 59, pp. 664-687.

Ms. Magazine
1972   Letters. July, p. 43.

Newcomb, W. W. Jr.
1950   "A Re-examination of the Causes of Plains Warfare," *American Anthropologist*, vol. 52, pp. 317-330.

1960   "Toward an Understanding of War," in *Essays in the Science of Culture in Honor of Leslie A. White* (Crowell Co., N.Y.) pp. 317-336.

Newsletter of the American Anthropological Association
1972   Letters. June, vol. 13, no. 6 (American Anthropological Association, Washington, D.C.).

Penthouse Magazine
1971   Interview with Germain Greer. September, p. 52.

Peretz, E., R. W. Goy, C. H. Phoenix, and J. A. Resko
1971   "Influence of Gonadal Hormones on the Development and Activation of the Nervous System of the Rhesus Monkey," in *Influence of Hormones on the Nervous System,* D.H. Ford, ed. (S. Karger, N.Y.), pp. 401-411.

Playboy Magazine
1972   Interview with Germaine Greer. January.

Psychology Today
1972   "Sisterhood is Beautiful, A Coversation with Alice S. Rossi." August, pp. 40-46, 72-75.

1972   "Tie Line." August, p. 16.

Reiss, Ira L.
1960   *Premarital Sexual Standards in America* (The Glencoe Free Press of Glencoe, New York).

Relkin, Richard
1971   "Absence of Alteration in Puberal Onset in Male Rats following Amygdaloid Lesioning," *Endocrinology,* vol. 88, pp. 1272-1274.

Rosenblum, L.
1961   "The Development of Social Behavior in the Rhesus Monkey." Unpublished doctoral dissertation (University of Wisconsin Libraries, Madison).

Rosenblum, L. A. and R. D. Nadler
1971 "The Ontogeny of Sexual Behavior in Male Bonnet Macaques" in *Influence of Hormones on the Nervous System*, D. H. Ford, ed. (S. Karger, New York), pp. 388-400.

Sacks, Karen
1970 "Social Basis for Sexual Equality: A Comparative View" in *Sisterhood is Powerful*, Robin Morgan, ed. (Vintage Books, New York), pp. 455-469.

Saturday Review
1971 "Woman's Place in the Curriculum," by Janice Law Trecker. October 16, p. 83.

1972 "On Leaving New York" (editorial signed by Ronald P. Kriss). September 2, p. 24.

Scacchi, P., J. A. Moguilevsky, C. Libertun, and J. Christot
1970 "Sexual Differences in Protein Content of the Hypothalamus in Rats," *Proc. of the Society for Experimental Biology and Medicine*, vol. 133, pp. 845-848.

Science News
1972 "Social and Sexual Influences on Testosterone," April 29, p. 281.

1972 "Testosterone Levels under Stress," May 20, p. 331.

Scientific American
1972 "Science and the Citizen: Petite Difference," August, p. 46.

Service, Elman K.
1962 *Primitive Social Organization* (Random House, New York).

Shelly, Martha
1970 "Notes of a Radical Lesbian," in *Sisterhood is Powerful*, Robin Morgan, ed. (Vintage Books, New York), pp. 306-311.

Sherfey, Mary Jane
1970 "A Theory on Female Sexuality," in *Sisterhood Is Powerful,* Robin Morgan, ed. (Vintage Books, New York), pp. 220-230. (Reprinted from *Journal of the American Psychoanalytic Association,* vol. 14, pp. 28-128.)

Smith, Stuart L. and Cynthia Sauder
1969   "Food Cravings, Depression, and Premenstrual Problems," *Psychosomatic Medicine*, vol. 31, pp. 281-287.

Solanis, Valerie
1970   "Excerpts from the SCUM (Society for Cutting up Men) Manifesto" from *Sisterhood is Powerful*, Robin Morgan, ed. (Vintage Books, New York), pp. 514-519.

Soriero, Olive and D. H. Ford
1971   "Age and Sex: The Effect on the Composition of Different Regions of the Neonatal Rat Brain," in *Influence of Hormones on the Nervous System,* D.H. Ford, ed. (S. Karger, N.Y.), pp. 322-333.

Spiro, M. E.
1956   *Kibbutz: Venture in Utopia* (Harvard University Press, Cambridge).

1958   *Children of the Kibbutz* (Harvard University Press, Cambridge).

Statistical Abstract of the United States
1971   U. S. Department of Commerce (U. S. Government Printing Office, Washington, D.C.).

Steinem, Gloria
1972   Interview, *Redbook Magazine*, January, pp. 69-76.

Stewart, J.M.
1972   *Denver Post,* July 24.

Swanson, Ethel M. and David Foulkes
1968   "Dream Content and the Menstrual Cycle," *The Journal of Nervous and Mental Disease*, vol. 145, pp. 358-363.

Tholen, John F.
1970   "A Model of Homosexuality and Hypoadrenocorticism: Some Cultural and Physiological Factors" (Unpublished paper prepared for course in School Public Health at UCLA).

Tinbergen, Niko
1971   *Animal Behavior* (Time-Life Books, New York), p. 174.

Tintera, John W.
1968 "Hypoadrenocorticism" (Hypoglycemia Foundation, Scarsdale, N.Y.).

United Nations
1970 *Demographic Yearbook of the United Nations*, 22nd issue (United Nations, New York).

Wallace, Anthony F. C.
1970 *Culture and Personality* (Random House, N.Y.).

Ward, Ingeborg L.
1972 "Prenatal Stress Feminizes and Demasculinizes the Behavior of Males," *Science*, January 7, vol. 175, pp. 82-84.

Weller, George W. and Richard Q. Bell
1965 "Basal Skin Conductance and Neonatal State," *Child Development*, vol. 36, pp. 647-657.

White, Leslie A.
1949 *The Science of Culture* (Grove Press, N.Y.).

Whiting, John W. M.
1961 "Socialization Process and Personality," in *Psychological Anthropology: Approaches to Culture and Personality*, Francis L. K. Hsu, ed. (The Dorsey Press, Homewood, Ill.), pp. 355-380.

Young, Allen
1971 "A Gay Manifesto," *Ramparts*, November, pp. 50-59.

Young, Frank W.
1962 "The Function of Male Initiation Ceremonies: A Cross-Cultural Test of an Alternative Hypothesis," *American Journal of Sociology*, vol. LXVII, p. 380.

Bibliography

Abbott, Sidney and Barbara Soal
1972   *Sappho Was A Right-On Woman: A Liberated View of Lesbianism* (Stein and Day, New York).

Adams, Elsie and Mary Louis Briscoe
1971   *Up Against the Wall Mother . . . on Women's Liberation* (Glencoe Press, Beverly Hills, Calif.).

Addis, Margaret E.
1970   *Problems of Administrative Change in Selected Programs for the Reeducation of Women.* Thesis accepted at Harvard University, 1967. (Ann Arbor: University Microfilms).

Albrecht, Margaret
1967   *A Complete Guide for the Working Mother* (Doubleday, Garden City, New York).

Alto
1971   *Burn This and Memorize Yourself* (Times Change Press, 1023 Sixth Ave., N.Y.).

American Academy of Political and Social Science
1914   *Annals.* vol. 56, no. 145.

1968   *Annals.* vol. 375, January.

American Journal of Sociology
1973   Changing Women in a Changing Society. Special Issue, January.

Astin, Helen S.
1969   *The Women Doctorate in America; Origins, Career, and Family.* (Russell Sage Foundation, New York).

Atlantic Monthly
1971   Articles by Catherine Drinker Bowen, Alice Rossi, Elizabeth Janeway, etc., vol. 225, no. 3, March.

Bardwick, Judith M., Elizabeth Douvan, Martina S. Homer, David Gutman
1970   *Feminine Personality and Conflict* (Brooks/Cole Publishing, Belmont, Calif.).

Bardwick, Judith M.
1971   *Psychology of Women: A Study of Bio-Cultural Conflicts* (Harper & Row, New York).

Barnard, T. H.
1971   "Conflict between state, protective legislation and federal laws prohibiting sex discrimination: is it resolved?" *Wayne Law Review*, vol. 17, January-February, pp. 25-65.

Beauvoir, Simone de
1952   *The Second Sex* (Knopf, New York).

1969   *The Woman Destroyed* (Putnam and Sons, New York).

Benston, Margaret
n.d.   *The Political Economy of Women's Liberation* (New England Free Press, Boston).

Bird, Caroline
1970   *Born Female: The High Cost of Keeping Women Down,* rev. ed. (McKay, New York).

Boserup, Ester
1970   *Woman's Role in Economic Development* (St. Martin's Press, New York).

Brecher, Ruth and Edward, ed.
1966   *An Analysis of Human Sexual Response* (Little, Brown, Boston).

Brown, Barbara, Thomas Emerson, Gail Falk, and Ann E. Freedman
1971   "The Equal Rights Amendment: A constitutional basis for equal rights for women." *The Yale Law Journal*, vol. 80, no. 5, p. 871, April.

Brown, Donald R., ed.
1968   *The Role and Status of Women in the Soviet Union* (Teachers College Press, New York).

Business Weekly
1971   "Japanese women join the lib movement," pp. 70-72, April 10.

Caldwell, B.M., S. Boyer and J. Black
1971   "Day care." *Saturday Review,* vol. 54, pp. 47-53, February 20.

Chisholm, Shirley
1970   *Unbought and Unbossed* (Houghton Mifflin, Boston).

Colon, Clara
1970   *Enter, Fighting; Today's Woman, a Marxist-Leninist View* (New Outlook, New York).

Conway, J.
1970   "Stereotypes of femininity in a theory of sexual evolution." *Victorian Studies,* vol. 14, pp. 47-62, September.

Cooke, Joanne
1970   *A Motive Anthology on Women's Liberation* (The Bobbs-Merrill Co., Inc., New York).

Cott, Nancy F., ed.
1972   *Root of Bitterness* (Dunton, New York).

Dannett, Sylvia
1964   *Profiles of Negro Womanhood* (M.W. Lads, New York).

Decter, Midge
1971   *The Liberated American and Other Americans* (Coward, McCann & Geoghegen, Inc., New York).

deFord, Miriam Allen
1971   "Women Against Themselves: a sizeable proportion of articulate American women honestly believe that they are inferior. . ." *Humanist,* vol. 31, pp. 8-9, January-February.

DeRham, Edith
1965   *The Love Fraud; Why the Structure of the American Family is Changing and What Women Must do to Make it Work* (Potter, New York).

Devlin, Bernadette
1969   *The Price of My Soul* (Knopf, New York).

Diner, Helen
1965   *Mothers and Amazons: the First Feminine History of Culture* (Julian Press, New York).

Dixon, Marlene
1971-2   "Public ideology and the class composition of women's liberation." *Berkeley Journal of Sociology,* vol. 16, pp. 148-167.

Eastern Michigan University
1971   *The Role of Women in Society* Bibliography Series Number Twenty. Prepared by Hannelore B. Roder and Mary Butterfield.

Ellmann, Mary
1968   *Thinking About Women* (Harcourt, New York).

Engels, Friedrich
1942   *The Origin of the Family, Private Property and the State in Light of the Researches of Lewis H. Morgan* (International, New York).

Farber, Seymour M. and Roger, H. L. Wilson, eds.
1963   *Man and Civilization: the Potential of Woman. A Symposium* (McGraw-Hill, New York).

Ferguson, Charles
1966   *The Male Attitude* (Little, Brown, Boston).

Ferriss, Abbott L.
1971   *Indicators of Trends in the Status of American Women* (Russell Sage Foundation, New York).

Figes, Eva
1970   *Patriarchal Attitudes* (Stein and Day, Boston).

Firestone, Shulamith
1970   *The Dialectic of Sex; the Case for a Feminist Revolution* (Morrow, New York).

Friedan, Betty
1963   *The Feminine Mystique* (Norton, New York).

Gornick, Vivian and Barbara K. Morgan, eds.
1971   *Women in Sexist Society; Studies in Power and Powerlessness* (Basic Books, New York).

Hacker, Helen M.
1971   "Why can't a woman . . . ?" *Humanist*, vol. 31, pp. 10-13, January-February.

Harding, Mary Esther
1970   *The Way of All Women. A Psychological Interpretation* (G. P. Putnam's Sons, New York).

Harris, Ann Sutherland
1970   "The second sex in academe," *AAUP Bulletin*, vol. 56, pp. 283-95, September.

Hole, Judith and Ellen Levine
1971   *Rebirth of Feminism* (Quadrangle Books, New York).

Hughes, Marija M.
1970   *The Sexual Barrier: Legal and Economic Aspects of Employment* (San Francisco).

Kanowitz, Leo
1968   *Women and the Law; The Unfinished Revolution* (University of New Mexico Press, Albuquerque).

Kraditor, Aileen S.
1968   *Up From the Pedestal: Selected Writings in the History of American Feminism* (Quadrangle, Chicago).

Leffler, Ann and Dair L. Gillespie
1971-2   "A feminist reply: we deny the allegations and defy the allegator." *Berkeley Journal of Sociology*, vol. 16, pp. 168-179.

Leonard, Eugenie, and others
1962   *American Woman in Colonial and Revolutionary Times, 1565-1800: A Syllabus with Bibliography* (University of Pennsylvania Press, Philadelphia).

Lifton, Robert J., ed.
1965   *The Woman in America* (Houghton-Mifflin, Boston).

Mailer, Norman
1971   *The Prisoner of Sex* (Little, Brown, Boston).

Marx, Karl, et al.
1950   *Women and Communism* (Lawrence and Wishart, London).

Masters, William L. and Virginia Johnson
1966   *Human Sexual Responses* (Little, Brown, Boston).

1970   *Human Sexual Inadequacy* (Little, Brown, Boston).

Mattfeld, Jaquelyn A. and Carl G. Vanaken
1965   *Women and the Scientific Professions* (Institute of Technology Press, Cambridge, Mass.).

McGuigan, Dorothy G.
1970   *A Dangerous Experiment. 100 Years of Women at the University of Michigan* (Ann Arbor Center for Continuing Education of Women).

Mead, Margaret
1963   *Sex and Temperament in Three Primitive Societies* (Morrow, New York).

Messer, Mary B.
1928   *The Family in the Making, An Historic Sketch* (Putnam, New York).

Millett, Kate
1970   *Sexual Politics* (Doubleday, Garden City, New York).

Mishima, Sumie S.
1971   *The Broader Way. A Woman's Life in the New Japan* (Greenwood Press, Westport, Conn.).

Morgan, Elaine
1972   *The Descent of Woman* (Stein and Day, New York).

New Republic
1971   "Double Standard." Vol. 164, pp. 12-15, May 29.

O'Neill, William L.
1969   *Everyone Was Brave: The Rise and Fall of Feminism in America* (Quadrangle, Chicago).

1969   *The Woman Movement. Feminism in the United States and England* (George Allen and Unwin Ltd., London).

Ossoli, Sarah M.
1968   *Woman in the Nineteenth Century and Kindred Papers Relating to the Sphere, Condition, and Duties of Woman* (Greenwood, New York).

Patai, Raphael
1967   *Women in the Modern World* (Free Press, New York).

Rainwater, Lee
1960   *And the Poor Get Children; Sex, Contraception and Family Planning in the Working Class* (Quadrangle, Chicago).

Reed, Evelyn
1971   *Problems of Women's Liberation: a Marxist Approach*, 5th ed. (Pathfinder Press, New York).

Riegel, Robert E.
1963   *American Feminists* (University of Kansas Press, Lawrence).

1970   *American Women: A Story of Social Change* (Fairleigh Dickinson University Press, Rutherford).

Rollin, Betty
1971   "Backlash against women's lib! They're a bunch of frustrated hags." *Look*, vol. 35, pp. 15-16, March 9.

Ross, Nancy W.
1944   *Westward the Women* (Knopf, New York).

Rukeyser, W. S.
1971   "Corporate care for the kids." *Fortune*, vol. 84, pp. 104-109, September.

Schaffter, Dorothy
1948   *What Comes of Training Women for War* (American Council on Education, Washington).

Schur, Edwin M.
1964   *The Family and the Sexual Revolution; Selected Readings* (Indiana University Press, Bloomington, Indiana).

Scott, Anne, ed.
1971   *The American Woman: Who Was She?* (Prentice-Hall, Englewood Cliffs, New Jersey).

Sherfey, Mary Jane
1972   *The Nature and Evolution of Female Sexuality* (Random House, New York).

Sullerot, Evelyne
1971   *Woman, Society, and Change* (McGraw-Hill, New York).

Summer, H. L.
1971   "Historical development of women's work in the United States." *Academy of Political Sciences. Proceedings,* vol. 30, pp. 101-113, May.

Thompson, Mary Lou, ed.
1970   *Voices of the New Feminism* (Beacon, Boston).

U. S. Senate
1970   Subcommittee on Constitutional Amendments of Committee on the Judiciary. *Hearings.* The Equal Rights Amendment. Washington, May (Y4.J89/2/6/970).

Wollstonecraft, Mary
        A Vindication of the Rights of Women (Scott, London). Originally published in 1797.

Women: A Journal of Liberation